CHASING THE SHADOW
—THE WORLD AND ITS TIMES

CHASING THE SHADOW
—THE WORLD AND ITS TIMES

An Introduction to Christian Natural Theology, Volume 2

Ephraim Radner

CASCADE *Books* • Eugene, Oregon

CHASING THE SHADOW—THE WORLD AND ITS TIMES
An Introduction to Christian Natural Theology, Volume 2

Copyright © 2018 Ephraim Radner. All rights reserved. Except for brief quotations in critical publications or reviews, no part of this book may be reproduced in any manner without prior written permission from the publisher. Write: Permissions, Wipf and Stock Publishers, 199 W. 8th Ave., Suite 3, Eugene, OR 97401.

Cascade Books
An Imprint of Wipf and Stock Publishers
199 W. 8th Ave., Suite 3
Eugene, OR 97401

www.wipfandstock.com

Unless otherwise indicated, Scripture quotations are taken from the King James Version. Other Scripture quotations are taken from the Revised Standard Version of the Bible, copyright © 1952 by the Division of Christian Education of the National Council of the Churches of Christ in the United States of America. Used by permission. All rights reserved.

PAPERBACK ISBN: 978-1-5326-3004-0
HARDCOVER ISBN: 978-1-5326-3006-4
EBOOK ISBN: 978-1-5326-3005-7

Cataloguing-in-Publication data:

Names: Radner, Ephraim, author.

Title: Chasing the shadow—the world and its times : an introduction to Christian natural theology, volume 2 / Ephraim Radner.

Description: Eugene, OR : Cascade Books, 2018 | Includes bibliographical references.

Identifiers: ISBN 978-1-5326-3004-0 (paperback : volume 2) | ISBN 978-1-5326-3006-4 (hardcover : volume 2) | ISBN 978-1-5326-3005-7 (ebook : volume 2) | ISBN 978-1-60899-017-7 (paperback : volume 1)

Subjects: LCSH: 1. Poetry—21st century—Collections. | Natural Theology.

Classification: BT75.3 .R33 2018 (print) | BT75.3 .R33 (ebook)

Manufactured in the U.S.A.   APRIL 20, 2018

To A., H., and I., time's gifts

Table of Contents

Acknowledgements ix

Preface: Natural Theology and the Bible 1

POEMS 39

    Acrostic Time 39
    Accounting Time 40
    Adult Time 41
    Anniversary Time 43
    Baking Time 44
    Beautiful Time 46
    Birth Time 47
    Bone Time 48
    Cat Time 50
    Child Time 51
    Church Time 54
    Confession Time 56
    David's Time 57
    Demonic Time 59
    Dog Time 61
    Drunken Time 63
    Earth Time 64
    Family Time 66
    Friendship Time 67
    Growing up Time 68
    Historical Time 70
    Interfaith Time 71
    Jerusalem Time 73

Table of Contents

    Knowledge Time 74
    Marriage Time 75
    Mining Time 80
    Peace Time 82
    Prayer Time 83
    Prophet Time 84
    Rock Time 85
    Sea Time 87
    Stroke Time 89
    Suffering Time 91
    Suicide Time 92
    Summer Time 93
    Theodicy Time 94
    Torture Time 95
    Utah Time 96
    Victory Time 98
    War Time 99
    Weary Time 100
    Widow's Time 101
    Lenten Time 102
    Easter Time 120

Bibliography 125

Acknowledgements

Portions of the opening essay were written in conjunction with the Downey Lectures I gave at Ambrose University, Calgary, in October 2016. My deep thanks to Ambrose for the honor and opportunity afforded by that invitation. Several individual poems have appeared in *The Living Church*; my thanks to Christopher Wells, the editor, for his ongoing friendship and for the collegial ministry we share. The series on "Lenten Time" grew out of a Holy Week spent at Queens College, St. John's, Newfoundland, in 2015. I am grateful for their hospitality and the chance to teach there. I have learned much on Christian natural theology from the research and conversations of several students, especially David Ney and Jeff Boldt. Finally, my continued thanks to my wife, Annette, for her ongoing encouragement and patience in this and in all the work we share.

Preface: Natural Theology and the Bible

Natural theology has suffered a chequered career in the last two hundred years. In general, the phrase refers to a discipline of knowledge and speech: describing God truly, in some fashion, through a true description of the world that God has made. By the eighteenth century, natural theology in this sense was flourishing. With the expanding realm of modern science pressing into ever novel directions, each new discovery seemed to ornament the wisdom and greatness of God with burgeoning extravagance.[1] It was not exactly clear, though, how the developing science was actually deepening our knowledge of God. With a certain dismay, natural theologians watched as, in fact, God's particular character became increasingly overlain by the natural phenomena, to the point that his personality began to fade into the "laws" scientists were eagerly formulating and explicating. By the end of the nineteenth century, scientists themselves saw little that "theology" had to add to their work, and theologians themselves, perhaps in a kind of corporate disappointment, decided that "science" itself had little to do with theology, and that the "natural world" that science purported to describe had little to add. As a discipline, "natural theology" tended to be seen as corruptive of both a proper understanding of nature and a proper understanding of God.

There have been exceptions to this general trend. Both liberal and conservative Christian apologists, for example, have lamented the intellectual divide between "science and religion." Attuned to the shrinking purchase of theological understanding on Western culture more generally, these apologists have attempted to find ways of holding the two together. Liberal natural theologies, in this apologetic mode, have tended to embrace evolutionary or process visions of reality, including of God; conservative apologists, for their part, have tried to dissect scientific theory for areas

---

1. One of the most appealing, influential, and popular examples is John Ray's *The Wisdom of God* (1691), which went through over a dozen editions in the next century.

vulnerable to theistic causality and hence essential explication.[2] Compared to the traditional thrust of natural theology, which aimed at deepening our sense of the world's meaning as creature, and of God's as creator, these modern apologetic natural theologies have offered little that has enriched our spirits in the face of divine life. They have instead turned Christian claims into reflections of contemporary materialistic frameworks of explanation, from one perspective or another.

Yet the traditional task of natural theology remains compelling. In the first volume of this introduction, I offered four arguments.[3] First, I suggested generally that natural theology is an inevitable pursuit. That is because, second, it is bound to the receipt of our limits of creaturely existence, and hence deals with God, not directly, but as the metaphysical "shadow" that divine life casts upon creaturely existence: fundamental aspects of our created existence, most often experienced in terms of our limitations (including mortality), turn us to God. Third, I argued that the creative and deepening character of natural theology lies in the way this description of God's shadowed reality encounters and engages the divine self-offering that is given in revelation, the Scriptures of Christ. Finally, I indicated that this encounter is often best described in poetic, rather than logically discursive, terms, precisely because of poetry's rootedness in mimetic articulation— the "world as it is," the "world in the shadow of God."

In this volume I want to explore aspects of this general argument more specifically, by focusing on that aspect of natural existence that we engage through our temporal limitations. I believe that the mimetic particularities of poetic description that suitably articulate the creaturely character of the world are most evident in their temporal subordination to divine revelation itself. Poetry, in its non-systematic, non-comprehensive, and discrete focus, as well as in its similarly non-coercive imagistic associations, best reflects the way that God orders creaturely life—the natural world. When made the vehicle of encounter with revelation—an encounter that is intrinsic to natural *theology*—poetry then discloses created life as it is temporally put into play or used by God, a use that is multiple, often dislocated according to

---

2. The "process" side has moved from pneumatological versions like Charles Raven's prototypical *The Creator Spirit* to more theoretically adaptive versions like the bestselling book by Paul Davies, *God and the New Physics*. More conservative Christian apologetics, with its attempt to wed aspects of evolution with theistic "design," is exemplified in the geneticist Francis Collin's BioLogos Foundation and its work; see http://biologos.org/about-us/.

3. Radner, *World in the Shadow of God*.

quantifiable temporal schemes, and essentially dependent on the purposes of God, which only Scripture can fully present. The paradox of temporality as an essential aspect of createdness is that its theological importance unveils temporality's own intrinsic incoherence. A faithful Christian natural theology will both attend to temporality's inescapable details and discover that these details escape the orbit of "natural" time as they are ordered by the gravity of their originating Scriptures.

The bulk of the present essay, then, is devoted to reflecting on this subordinate relationship of experienced temporality to Scripture's creative form. This will constitute a reflection standing alongside the poems that engage in a natural theology founded on some of these presuppositions, although its theoretical posture is not to be confused with the character of natural theology itself.

The presuppositions, however, are important. Their articulation derives from a variety of activities, including simply doing natural theology. Most important is the definition of Scripture as the divine ordering of the created world given by God to human beings in the form of a specific linguistic document. This is not meant to be an exhaustive or final definition, but it is one that arises from describing the world in the shadow of the God revealed in Christ Jesus; hence, the definition is both "built into" the gospel and utterly concrete. My concern is that, in the Christian church—even conservative churches—we have been more and more forgetting how to read Scripture the way it has, in some fashion or another, always been read: as God's great informer of our lives and world. Scripture is a divine agency, even an agent. By contrast, we now tend to read Scripture as a set of instructions, a legal document of a sort. The problem with reading the Bible this way, even if one thinks that the law it offers is "right," is that eventually that law will be questioned: new situations, special circumstances, changed needs. In such new situations, one might then look for the "spirit of the law," so that even if the law changes its basic orientation is maintained. This move represents the liberal drift of all Scripture reading. Finally, however, and as with all legal systems, one must throw the whole thing out altogether, and start all over. The world is full of nations, from Estonia to Ecuador, who have done just this with their legal systems in the last two decades. Churches and their members are also increasingly prey to such an outcome.

But what if Scripture is not like a legal document at all? What if Scripture actually *constitutes* the world, *makes* the world what the world in fact is, from the bottom up? Certainly, it is a different kind of reading of Scripture that would bear this out, and it is a kind of reading that has characterized Christian natural theology for centuries. We can get at this tradition, and at the definition of Scripture that derives from it, by first asking how things "happen" in the world. I will end this first section of the essay by suggesting that everything happens "according to Scripture," that is, that the world is scripturally ordered. In the second section, I will take up this general conclusion, and reflect on some aspects of what this might mean for understanding the world more broadly—what I will call a scriptural natural theology. If everything happens according to Scripture, how might we look at the world?

I. TIME AS GOD'S GIVING OF THE WORLD

1. *God of the Living*

Most readers of early modern philosophy are familiar with the famous religious experience that the mathematician Blaise Pascal had when he was thirty-one. It is famous now, although until he died it was a secret. He wrote about it on a small bit of paper that he kept sewn into his coat lining and carried with him at all times. Only when he was dead did they find it. The paper noted the date—November 23, 1654—and the hours—10:30 p.m. to 12:30 p.m. Now known as the *Mémorial*, the opening words of this scrap of paper are now celebrated: "Fire. God of Abraham, God of Isaac, God of Jacob. Not of philosophers and scholars. Certainty, certainty, heartfelt, joy, Peace. God of Jesus Christ . . ."[4] The opening line is often identified as a quote from Exodus 3:6, which of course it is. But it is also a quote from Matthew 22:32, where Jesus quotes Exodus, and then adds, "not the God of the dead, but of the living." Not the God of philosophers, scholars, or of the dead, but of the living: of Abraham, Isaac, and Jacob.

A key element of the *Mémorial* is the way Pascal insists that the people of the past are alive. They are alive "to" God, or better "by" God and "in" God. Pascal also ends his meditation about the immediacy of God with a quote from Psalm 119:16: "I will not forget your word"—*non obliviscar sermones tuos*, in the Latin Vulgate he scribbles down. God is God of those, from the past, who are living, in a way that is founded by Scripture itself. How can that be? How can a text that tells us how people die *also* found our encounter with the God for whom those dead persons are in fact alive? That

---

4. Pascal, *Pensées*, 311.

could only be the case if that text—Scripture—were tied to the very creative acts themselves of God. That is, in fact, the assumption that Pascal then works with in his subsequent writing: Scripture itself "makes" the world—its peoples, its events, their choices, their destinies. Scripture is *how* God, in Christ, creates; Scripture is also how God recreates. Hence, the world, in all of its natural objects and realities, literally belongs to Scripture.

I believe that one of the key elements that has accompanied the demise of Scripture's plausibility, let alone authority, in the contemporary era has been the decoupling of Scripture from the natural world, including the breadth of our temporal experience. The creationism-evolution debate has been but a reactive response to that decoupling. That particular debate has proven unilluminating because it has been pursued on the playing field of the secular natural sciences, rather than on a larger canvas of divine reality. Within the evolution debate, that is, the Bible has been read in terms of historical-scientific discourse, rather than the world being read as a reflection of the God who speaks scripturally. There is a difference, as I will indicate: the world and its happenings looks like Scripture; Scripture does not look like the world's a-theistically described history or science. Scripture really is the living God creating and working in the world.

2. The Historical Vagaries of Natural Theology

Natural theology is the discipline or practice that aims at learning something or saying something true about God on the basis of the world in which we live. The traditional idea undergirding what became the discipline of natural theology was that, if God is the creator of all things, then we can know something about God by examining what God has made, that is, the natural world, including our own selves as creatures. We can look at the "way" of living organisms, perhaps their shape and activities; we can study the stars or the orbits of the planets; we can scrutinize the character of human thought and language. In doing all these things, we shall learn something true, perhaps deeply true, about God.

From a Christian perspective, the claim to natural theology was almost always linked to a claim about the coherence of such theology with the truths of revelation, preeminently of Scripture. This coherence was taken for granted for centuries: there were "two books" from which we might know God, the book of Scripture and the book of Nature.[5] In general, prac-

---

5. Pedersen, *Book of Nature*. More specialized studies can be found in van der Meer and Mandelbrote, *Nature and Scripture in the Abrahamic Religions*.

tical priority was given to the former. After all, the reality of the gospel, in its articulate commands and teachings and in its historical narrative, could only be found in an articulate human language, such as that recorded in the Bible. The world of the tadpole and frog could not tell us of Christ, at least in any very specific way. Still, the "at least" here was never cut off from the reality of the pond and its inhabitants: one might, many thought, observe the pond and see something pressing towards the truth of Christ within its forms; and, having known Christ in his scriptural figures, one was not only able but also morally compelled to see these figures within the teeming waters of the marsh and lake. The world was a "book" written by God and speaking about God: "In your great wisdom you, who are our God, speak to us of these things in your Book, the firmament made by you."[6]

Some of the fullest Christian pursuits of natural theology in this vein engaged a kind of Neoplatonic metaphysic that allowed thinkers to assume that material creatures, in their forms, could be meditatively followed "up," as it were, to their higher exemplars within God's creative mind. There was a kind of spiritual ascent that the Christian could engage in looking at the natural world, and this ascent would lead to a clearer and more brilliant contemplation upon the very face of God, from whom all things come, and of Christ in particular, in whom, and by whom, and for whom all things were made (see Col 1:16–17). The work of the medieval Franciscan St. Bonaventure is typical of this view.[7] But long before this more elaborated mystical program, theologians as diverse as Basil of Caesarea or Augustine himself had worked with this idea in the background of their assumptions.[8] They saw Romans 1:20, at least, as a clear warrant for their views: "For the invisible things of him from the creation of the world are clearly seen, being understood by the things that are made, [even] his eternal power and Godhead; so that they are without excuse."

Nonetheless, a Neoplatonic metaphysic was not a necessary presupposition for Christian natural theology of this kind. More fundamentally, and more widely, the belief in God as the sole creator of all things was sufficient to ground a conviction in the revelatory character of creation itself.[9] When this was joined, as it always was, to a belief in the divine character of Scripture itself, the natural world was always viewed in terms of a

---

6. Augustine, *Confessions*, 13.18.
7. See his *Itinerarium mentis ad Deum*.
8. See Radner, *Time and the Word*, 47–58.
9. Ibid., 111–62.

"language" by which God expressed or communicated his being and will. Because Scripture itself unveiled the creative work of God, that creative work, including the forms of the natural world, was explicated in terms of a language. Hence, two senses were joined into one here: to "look" at the world is to "hear" God speak; and to "hear" God speak, as in the Scriptures, is to "see" the world in its true form.

The Protestant Reformation upheld this view, as in the 1561 Belgic Confession (art. 2): "We know him [God] by two means: First, by the creation, preservation, and government of the universe, since that universe is before our eyes as a most elegant book in which all creatures, great and small, are as so many characters [*lettres*] leading us to contemplate *the invisible things of God* . . ."[10] By contrast, the modern world has moved towards a division of these two senses: the "visual" and the "oral/aural." Cultural historians have traced this division at various moments,[11] but the outcome has been to undermine the plausibility of natural theology as a practice. Where, in classical Christian exegesis, the typological reading of Scripture was bound to a habit of seeing the world and its temporal life as God-ordered and hence revelatory, modern Christian habits have tended to separate history and its objects from the moral significance of the Bible's intellectual teaching.

It is at this point that natural theology began to wilt in Christian terms, beginning somewhere in the eighteenth century, and turning into a clear abandonment of natural theology by the later nineteenth century, at least by all but a few hangers-on. It is a complicated story.[12] But the nexus of change seems to have been located in this separation of "world" and "word." On the one hand, many Christian natural philosophers continued to see the objects of nature as divinely crafted. Yet the character of these objects became less and less bound by the words of Scripture themselves. What manifested the divine origin of the natural world were very specific characteristics that had little to do with biblical specificity (although they were hardly alien

---

10. In Schaff, ed., *Creeds of Christendom*, 384.

11. See Ong, *Orality and Literacy*; and McLuhan, *Gutenberg Galaxy*.

12. One cannot be too cut and dry about developments. See Eddy, "Nineteenth-Century Natural Theology," which underlines some of the remaining vigor in outlook and argument during the nineteenth century. But even here, Eddy writes, "there is no denying the more subdued presence of natural theology within Western educational settings as the new century moved forward" (113). Natural theology, where it flourished, did so in more popular devotional contexts rather than in the academy. See Macmillan, *Bible Teachings in Nature*; or Child, *Great Architect*.

to scriptural claims): order, usefulness, intricacy. If you could note these, you could safely say that God was at work. These were understood, in very precise ways, to be "principles" of creation, and natural theology came to be measured by its ability to articulate "laws," in a way that was finally taken over by non-theistic measures of scientific order. The Bible, on the other hand, as it became increasingly divorced from natural claims, was viewed as speaking mainly to moral realities: duties, responsibilities, and ordered motives. Mirroring the increasing value placed upon law-like frameworks, favored by the natural theologians of developing scientific modernity, these biblical topics tended themselves to be reduced into abstracted outlines of moral demand, but without any purchase on the actual forms of the world's concrete ordering. This is called reading the Bible "tropologically"—as a text that tells you how to act. Job tells us how to be patient; Jonah tells us how to be obedient; David tells us how to be repentant, and so on.

Not only were the "two books" of Scripture and Nature now seemingly divorced, but the character of the divorce exposed what had once been a key means of holding the two together. One way to describe the difference between pre-eighteenth-century classical Christian natural theology and the post-eighteenth-century dissolution of natural theology was the disappearance of history altogether as a realm of divine meaning. Much of the Christian tradition had insisted, after all, that it was history, as God's theater of creation, that brought Bible and nature together. Instead, whether tinctured with remnants of the fall or simply abandoned as an empty field of refuse, history by the seventeenth and eighteenth centuries became increasingly seen as a problem for theology. It was either the sum total of human mistakes or a piling up of otherwise arbitrary leftovers from nature and moral progress. Hence, for some thinkers, nature most clearly pointed to God when human beings were left out of the picture, and therefore scriptural detail was excluded from the purity of science. By contrast, many biblical theologians assumed that historical particularity could only sully the clarity of the divine law that lay behind the messy biblical documents. In either case, how could the world as it has *actually* confronted human beings speak of God? Finally, those philosophers, like Hegel, who still turned to history as a revelatory reality tended to divinize it wholly, something that thinned out the natural world and Scripture both.[13] Providential history

---

13. The rise of theodicy, by that name or its thematic cognates, set up a struggle with natural theology that finally left human contingency out of the mix altogether when it came to religious arguments—such that contingency became the province of nontheistic interests. Leibniz, Pope, and in his own way Voltaire generally worried through

Preface: Natural Theology and the Bible

was still very much a live understanding through the nineteenth century, as discussions of British (and American) international destiny demonstrate. But the foundations for this understanding had long been nibbled away at, and the First World War suddenly brought the edifice of Christian providentialism crashing down.[14]

The twentieth century inherited, then, three categories: a "natural world" bound finally to the laws of physics as they came to be articulated; a scriptural world, tied to the mental constructs of its variously committed theological readers, telling us how to be good; and a bloody human world, in which people do this and that, but which is best left ignored for the purposes of truth-seeking, or tidied up by pragmatic means for whatever moral conscience or human desire might grasp after. Perhaps God could be seen in the first category—the natural world—as a kind of icon of mysterious order, as Einstein wondered.[15] Perhaps God could be followed in the second category—the Bible as a book of moral instruction—insofar as theological commitments could express divine moral imperatives.[16] And perhaps God could be mercifully forgotten in the last category—the theater of history—since both order and moral imperative always seemed to dissipate within the vagaries of incomplete and failed efforts to sort out human action. (Progressive Christians, meanwhile, thought that God might be recovered for history if they just worked harder to make things better.)

Within the vying and often overlapping habits of each categorical experience, the created world itself, as a coherent language of God's own self, given in Christ, has simply vanished. Environmental fears in our own day have certainly fueled a desire among many Christian thinkers to link the earth with God, but mostly this is done on the level of ethical demand, not revelatory divine speech. (There are, of course, non-Christian responses that have divinized the planet itself, but this is another trajectory altogether.[17]) If

---

their theories in ways that ignored human particularity. Susan Neiman's *Evil in Modern Thought* is useful, if not in explicating the theological issues involved, at least in laying out some of the conceptual challenges and developments that seventeenth- and eighteenth-century philosophers engaged.

14. See generally Marrin, *Last Crusade*. Wilkinson, *Dissent or Conform* offers some specific theological discussions.

15. Einstein, *Ideas and Opinions*, 36–53.

16. The so-called culture wars in America, from the late twentieth century to the present, engage the Bible on this level. See Deckman and Prud'homme, *Curriculum and the Culture Wars*. Some of this is laid out in its complex context by the originator of the phrase, Hunter, in his *Culture Wars*.

17. So, for instance, the Gaia movement. See Primavesi, *Sacred Gaia*.

discussed in its traditional form, the very notion of a natural theology has necessarily been roundly rejected, on moral as much as on philosophical grounds, as an often dangerous impossibility: when we start claiming to know God from what we experience within these now incoherent realms of the world—from sand dunes to car accidents, forests to wars—we end by projecting our own finite and sometimes downright evil qualities upon God, apotheosizing our frustrations. Thereby, we divinize our own failures, and in the process we claim a power to impose them upon the world in a way that inevitably leads to disaster.

3. The Reflective Turn: Natural Theology's Phenomenological Basis

The purpose of this historical sketch is to show how we are today heirs of a set of spectacles. They provide us lenses that probably keep us from seeing some basic things. One major element, now obscured, is that simple self-reflection drives us to God. Not all Christians have been happy with this claim, especially among some Protestants—perhaps sin just perverts any Godward thought altogether. But I would claim, as I have done elsewhere,[18] that *at the least* a certain kind of self-reflection exposes us to, as it were, the underside of our existence before God. To exist is to know something about God, if only as the collision of our self-understanding with that unknown condition of possibility that lets us exist in the first place. Every difficult encounter of my life—what led Schopenhauer to claim finally that life itself is nothing *but* suffering, the pounding of fundamental cosmic energy against the meaninglessness of itself—presses upon me the question, "Why am I here at all?" And that question inevitably raises my gaze to God. There is no "reason" for me to be here, in a suffering world, as it were, apart from the "reason" behind all things, whether I can understand it or not. The world must be, at least, a "shadow" of that primordial reason. Hence, encounter with anything brings with it the power of God's own creative being: when I encounter one thing—whatever it may be, from a seashell to a person—the whole world comes to me as a possibility, because this one thing is the thing that God gives. It comes to be, it exists to encounter me, because of God—and in God are all things are "alive."

I am not simply making a theological statement here; I am trying to construe, theologically, the nature of our experience as human beings. We can say, theologically, that what we experience, in its identity, its shape, its contours, is "created by God." More fundamentally, we can say that what

---

18. Radner, *World in the Shadow of God*.

Preface: Natural Theology and the Bible

we experience is simply what there is when God acts, a kind of created residuum to God being God. The philosopher Jean-Luc Marion talks about experience as including in itself a "saturated" meaning that is divine; that is, there is always "more" to what we experience than we can explain positivistically.[19] I am suggesting the converse here: when God acts creatively and self-sufficiently, this world—and ourselves—is what we get. The famous argument of St. Anselm "proving" God's existence, the so-called ontological argument, is perhaps linked to this suggestion. Anselm argued that God is, by human definition, that greater than which nothing can be conceived, and existence must be included in such conceived greatness; therefore God exists.[20] It is an odd argument that has puzzled many for centuries. One way to look at it is in the self-reflective fashion I have just sketched: phenomena are God-indicating and, even more, God-derivative precisely in their mysterious contours and origins. We cannot ever get to their sources and ends. This is not simply a matter of needing more knowledge but lacking it; rather, it is a boundary character to human knowledge itself, to the fact of knowing something about ourselves as existent beings and about other objects within the world we encounter. Just to *think* "existence," and do so in the context of encountering other existing things—the world—is to come to a threshold of thought across which looms the reality of God.

As noted above, natural theology fell apart in the modern era, in part because historical experience—the order and set of things we encounter in life—seemed so meaningless when looked at on its own: wars, injustice, disease, hunger, loss of those we love; now throw in climate change. Nonetheless, reflecting on who we are at all leads us to recognize how even these realities exist as possibilities only because of the world existing as *from* somewhere else. We have trouble, to be sure, grasping what it all adds up to. But even to fail to grasp the whole is to sense the trembling resonance of what we do not hold: who *is* this Who has made us? To answer "no one has made us" is not an answer; it is turning away from the throbbing question that is unanswerable except by being confronted openly.

In fact, every thirteen-year-old asks these questions, and it is only the distraction of aging linked to our insistently distracting culture that has led many of us to find them beside the point. Taken as at least relevant questions, we can begin to see how our lives, as we live them out in all their questions and incompleteness and frustrations—these difficult encounters

---

19. Marion, *Being Given*, esp. 179–247.
20 Anselm, *Proslogion*, 7–8.

in the world—and just in their being lived out this way, are God-indicating. That means that history itself is God-indicating. The very reality of temporal extension—reaching out and seemingly in vain in the course of living—actually opens us to that which sustains, as it were, our gasping breath. This place of reaching out and not holding is where the "thingness" of the world comes to us. Everything tumbles into this space left by our blocked hopes. We see something, we sense it, bump into it precisely because we cannot see *everything* at once, or perhaps ever, even in sequence. We can view something—this room, other people, a road, a meal—only because it is *given* to us in this strange reality we call "existence." Without being "given," our world would be empty, and we ourselves would disappear. Alive, we know we are not the source of our life, whose impulsion comes from elsewhere, from outside our doing and often our asking: here it is, having come to us.

4. Temporality as Our Awakening to Divine Initiative

We can now turn to how we experience this "givenness" of our existence in an extended way, what we call history or time. Givenness is the compulsion of time, of living out our existence. That includes what we call past, present, and future: these are experienced aspects of divine encounter within creation. In terms of the negative or shadowed aspect of natural revelation, time becomes the vehicle of the creative residuum.

It is crucial to see this ontological bond between temporality and the upsurging into our sensibility of created being in its multiplicity and distinction, for this is the link back to the question of Scripture. We know created things as artifacts, God's own handiwork, because of their specificity as given from elsewhere—one thing after another, one in conjunction with another, gathered or scattered, arranged or falling upon each other, offerings to be taken or perhaps refused, reodered in our understandings, or left aside because of their incomprehensibility. The actual character of natural science, in its birthing from theological reflection, derives from this fundamental way in which temporal existence's shadowed life was understood to issue in objects, to be faced and studied. Somehow, early modern natural scientists said, things come to us in an *order* that we can map out. Hence, providence—the way God has ordered things to come to be and encounter us, one after another—became a facilitating category for observation in the seventeenth century, and natural "history" became a central form of natural "philosophy."[21]

21. For some rich discussion of this development and its complex avenues, see the

Preface: Natural Theology and the Bible

There are obvious problems that eventually arise over this growing emphasis on providence as the way we describe God's ordering of created phenomena. Samuel Clarke in the early eighteenth century was perhaps the most influential writer of his generation, and his influence extended well into the nineteenth century among natural scientists.[22] Clarke's specifically theological interests were focused on predictable laws of nature—he was a follower of Newton. This tended, however, to reduce God's relationship to the natural world to one of ordering wisdom. God is wise; the world and its physical being reflects that wisdom; scientists look to articulate it. But where was the Bible in all of this? Where were the particular forms of Israel's and Jesus's own history? These were slowly included in the frameworks of providential wisdom. History itself follows laws, scientific critics came to insist. These laws can be applied to peoples and cultures—laws, for instance, of religious development, e.g., from primitive sacrificial concepts to abstract moral consciousness.

Applying historical "laws" to the Bible allowed scholars to revisit distinctions present in the scriptural narratives that had previously been held captive to purely dogmatic construals. By the nineteenth century, this might mean that Israel was increasingly identified by many scholars with the items of an "Israelite history" or a history of the Near East.[23] It also meant that Judaism itself could be grasped as something more concrete than a dogmatic foil for Christian claims. Questions of election, faith, sin, repentance, promise, destruction, fulfilment—these had been standard categories with which one might read the Bible's history through the eighteenth century, but they no longer seemed to fit easily within the regularized schemata of providential history. It seemed better to read the history of Israel and the Gentiles in ways analogous to the development of geological or life forms. The providential matrix of the world's forms laid out

---

initial essays in Daston and Stolleis, eds., *Natural Law and Law of Nature*, especially those of Catherine Wilson and Friedrich Steinle.

22. Clarke's 1704 and 1705 Boyle Lectures were quickly published together and went through countless editions; see *A Discourse Concerning the Being and Attributes of God*, 5th ed. This work of Clarke was on the standard syllabus for undergraduates and then specifically divinity students in England, Ireland, and America well into the nineteenth century.

23. Some of these developments are discussed, through an examination of the career of eighteenth-century scholar Johann David Michaelis, in Legaspi, *Death of Scripture*. The movement reached its nineteenth-century apogee in the work of the Scottish scholar William Robertson Smith, whose *Lectures on the Religion of the Semites* became a standard in this "history of religions" approach to the Bible.

a place for Jew and Gentile to be apprehended as specific peoples whose experience in time was capable of examination and then reconsidered relationship. The rise of Christian Zionism, to take an instance of a highly theologically charged movement—something with its roots in the late seventeenth and eighteenth centuries—was possible in part only because Jews and Christians could increasingly be located as themselves corporate artifacts within a world populated by temporal, that is, historical, identities ordered by God.[24]

We can take another example: earthquakes were generally seen, even into the eighteenth century, as immediate acts of God's judgment and warning. John and Charles Wesley devoted a good deal of attention to this. But theirs was a disappearing viewpoint. By the mid-eighteenth century, Christian philosophers and theologians, including many American Protestants, were distinguishing God's larger purposes from the "secondary causes" that lay behind earthquakes—shifts in tides and geological structures—and the latter quickly took over all explanatory power: there was nothing to learn from earthquakes except how they followed the normal patterns of the earth's material laws.[25]

What disappeared in all this, of course, was the *particularity* of things, including, in this case, the rattling of the earth, in just this village; the crumbling of just *this* building; the wreckage of just *this* life. It was the "just-thisness," however, that scriptural natural theology had always upheld, through to its apogee just at the beginning of the seventeenth century. The great product of classic Christian natural theology was the "catalogue," that is, the simple listing of "things" or creatures. We see this in the book of Job and elsewhere in the Bible: long poetic lists, as in Job 38, of God's making of the planets, the seas, the clouds, the light and darkness, water, dirt, abysses, snow, winds, springs, rain, ice, stars; or in Psalm 104, with its trees, storks, lions, donkeys, and birds: "I know all the fowls of the mountains: and the wild beasts of the field [are] mine," God says in Psalm 50:11, and throughout Scripture we are given selections of this divine ownership in its reach.

---

24. On Christian Zionism's beginnings, see Lewis, *Origins of Christian Zionism*; and earlier Crome, *Restoration of the Jews*. On the new context's reformulating of religion historically, see Stroumsa, *New Science*.

25. John Wesley, *Hymns Occasioned by the Earthquake*; Charles Wesley, *Cause and Cure of Earthquakes*; Stout, *New England Soul*, 177–79, 259; Winthrop, *Lecture on Earthquakes*.

Preface: Natural Theology and the Bible

In the Middle Ages, these lists proliferated and were formalized often in amazing, if sometimes fanciful, detail.[26]

By the seventeenth century, this had grown into vast treatises of encyclopedic breadth on trees, and birds, and shells; on different kinds of rocks; and then, with increased global encounter, on peoples and cultures—all carefully and marvellously illustrated: the greatest books over produced.[27] These are now viewed as generally ignorant, for their classification systems were not ordered by what came to be seen as scientifically sound forms of classification—that is, "right" physical relations. What these showed instead were enumerations of the "given": classic paeans to created abundance and proliferation.

One thing to stress in this long Christian tradition is that the issue of "development" had no central interest; for the meaning of time was not immanent to its objects. We don't understand time according to some special linear ordering of created things. The meaning of time, instead, lay in the experience of givenness. Abundance, in fact, seems to be a characteristic of time itself, as more recent philosophers—e.g., Feyerabend, Deleuze, Serres—have stressed, an observation that goes back to St. Augustine's reflections on Genesis in the *Confessions* 13:24. That is simply because time is the experience of things being given to us, and we have no control over this givenness, its range, and constant flow. One could even describe time as the donative character of all reality. "Time" explains why things come and go, pass away, lose themselves before us—not so much in meaninglessness, but in the fact that these are not ours to order under our own steam. The poet Alfred Vigny once wrote that you can love only what you can never see twice: "*Aimez ce que jamais on ne verra deux fois.*"[28]

When we are conscious of the world around us, everything impresses itself upon our perception as something that is out of our control, in any consistent way. What is left in our consciousness, which is our temporal construal of God's gifts of all things, are the traces of "not-ours." This givenness, this "not-oursness," is the stuff out of which meaning arises. Mortality and disappearance, along with the uneven and usually feeble and final inadequacy of memory, are not in the first place marks of "vanity" or emptiness.

26. Hawkes, *Book of Nature*.

27. Among the great authors and artists involved in these productions: Leonhart Fuchs (1501–66), Conrad Gesner (1516–65), Robert Hooke (1635–1703), Bernard Picart (1673–1733), August Johann Rösel von Rosenhof (1705–59). See Kusukawa, "Illustrating Nature."

28. The poem "La maison du berger" first appeared in *Revue des Deux Mondes* (1844).

That's why a book like Ecclesiastes *is* "revelation": the very sadness embedded in the abundance of transient things of our world that come and go out of our grasp constitutes the divine residuum that reveals their origin. "I die, therefore God is," one could say, because my own coming and passing away reflect the fact that everything, myself included, is a gift.

A contemporary atheistic landscape, which has only things and cannot apprehend that things *mean* givenness—God giving—is always literally "at a loss": everything is eventually lost, first one at a time, and then in the cascade that terminates in the losing of our lives. Properly considered, however, temporality moves both chronologically and also constitutively towards the finding of that which is the only unlosable reality, who is God. A better way to put this, of course, is that this reality who is God is not so much the object of a finding, but is finding itself: "I understand as I am understood; I love, as I am loved; I find because I am found." That is Paul, in 1 Corinthinas 8(:3) and 13(:12). That is Jesus, in the whole fabric of his encouragement of his disciples to seek because first, as those who are lost, they have been sought after.

The fact that there is a world of things, of creatures, that we experience temporally is defined by God's initiative and grace utterly; and if everything is given by God, everything is divinely purposed. How do things "happen" in the world? They are given to us by God, according to his purpose. Things that happen, to be sure, are experienced by us through our construal of their coming and going as "time." We sense that things are given and have a place. This place need not be stable from our perspective. But having a place that is not our own, and that exists vis-à-vis our own, is something we cannot demand or manipulate. It comes to be before us as if "simply" given, and not as an order that arises from within things or is imposed by some reason that we hold as our own.

"Time," in this sense of things being given us, is a way of expressing the fact that all things come from God and are God's. To "have time" or "have a time" is a way of stating the fact that one exists only because God has made it so. I am not my own; I was bought at a price (see 1 Cor 6:20). Among other things, this statement of Paul means that I am a temporal being. This is a wholly theological claim, of course. The actual experience of time, which is only the articulated human self-consciousness of this reality, does not and certainly has not always included "God" as the condition for this consciousness. That condition, however, is not thereby annihilated on account of such a limitation.

Preface: Natural Theology and the Bible

There is a paradox at work in this realization as well: this reality that time is the frame of God-givenness is also time's undoing, for to have time is also to have the God whose time it is in a more primary way stand as our time *giver*, and thus to have more than time—or to have a time that is counted as such only because its being is given in the form of being counted. Our times, with their inherent frustrations and unfulfilled or limited extensions, "mean" or are constituted in their truth by that divine reality that stands towards time as "the eternal." Past, present, and future, as well as birthing, growing, dying, and disappearing, are all givens in this theological sense, and thus have a being that escapes their uncertain contours. Their significance lies in their relationship with eternality, with God himself.

Temporality, then, is the form that God's giving of created reality takes; it is the form in which creation is received and experienced by that which is created as just what it is. But this timely form of created reality is also *just* a form, whose actual meaning, as with any sign that indicates, is wrapped up with its linguistic agent, in this case with the eternal character of the Giver. The creature who grasps, or is grasped by, this indicating aspect of time, and by its ultimate referent—who, it turns out, does not stand apart from the sign but is its very condition for being—such a creature will be consciously thrust into a world whose objects and their relationships throb with divine meaning. Everything has a divine reason or order. That order is temporal, to be sure; but it is the orderedness from the God who constitutes time.

If providence is understood in its most basic sense, it describes this apprehension of divine orderedness that emerges for creatures as the ground of their apparent placement within the exhaustive relationship of temporal abundance. There is a range of ways one can talk about this. One might, for instance, call time a "function" of God's creative purpose in relation to creation. This would be analogous to the way William James could speak of the functionality of experience that is always given in relatedness. What we call consciousness, James argued, is the function of experience as it is known by a particular person; but "the world" and "consciousness" are in fact not two separate elements, but one thing—the "stuff" of reality—functioning in two ways.[29] For James this meant that everything is of a single piece, and his well-known monistic view of reality derives from this implication, as

---

29. James, *Essays in Radical Empiricism*, especially chapters 1 ("Does Consciousness Exist?") and 2 ("A World of Pure Experience").

well as his confidence that everything we engage—including religion—is somehow "real."

Why am I here, in this particular place and encountering these particular things? A Christian can take the idea of perspectival functions, but press it into the non-monistic reality of divine createdness and its ultimate distinction from God, as well as the diverse distinctions among creatures that make each unique. While diverse and distinct from God, however, the experience of a creature's life is a function of its life being ordered by God's holy will, desires, ideas, goodness, and being. Temporal experience is the deepest aspect of this created order.[30] In this sense, the term "use" is perhaps a more helpful one to apply to God's relationship with creatures in their temporal experience, because it contains, broadly, elements of intention, meaning, and performance all at once. When we say that "God uses" his creation, we rightly mean that God purposes that which he creates, and actively orders creatures according to this purpose. In this way, the "divine usefulness" or "usedness" of the world can be seen as its temporal being.[31]

The thirteen-year-old's question "Why am I here, in this particular place and encountering these particular things?" is simply answered: this is what God does. Created temporality, history, is the experienced appearance, the manifestation, of what God "does," of divine "doing." We are thus pressed into knowing God.

5. Scripture as the Shape of God's Doing

Here we can pass from the natural world to Scripture itself. For once we see creation as the form of God's doing, we are implicitly affirming that

---

30. The paragraph with which James ends his first essay is remarkable and bears quoting: "The 'I think' which Kant said must be able to accompany all my objects, is the 'I breathe' which actually does accompany them. There are other internal facts besides breathing (intracephalic muscular adjustments, etc., of which I have said a word in my larger Psychology), and these increase the assets of 'consciousness,' so far as the latter is subject to immediate perception; but breath, which was ever the original of 'spirit,' breath moving outwards, between the glottis and the nostrils, is, I am persuaded, the essence out of which philosophers have constructed the entity known to them as consciousness. *That entity is fictitious, while thoughts in the concrete are fully real. But thoughts in the concrete are made of the same stuff as things are*" (ibid., 37). That "breath" stands as our link to "reality"—the "function" of reality as it is "thought" by a creature—is a clear nod to the Genesis account of creation, even as it expresses itself in terms of the pneumatic monism that is the mark of modern metaphysics.

31. See Williams, "Language, Reality, Desire."

Preface: Natural Theology and the Bible

creation is the form or outworking of Scripture itself. For what God does, God speaks. That is, God's word is what God does.

To be sure, this is a specifically Christian (and Jewish) claim. From the perspective of such religious faith, however, it is a *natural* claim. Genesis 1:3 is the key text: "And God said, Let there be light: and there was light"—a founding divine agency bound up with the word/deed that is then alluded to in different ways in the course of the creation account. It is taken up again in texts that stress divine creation, but also in the New Testament, in terms of divine *re*creation.

> By the word of the LORD were the heavens made; and all the host of them by the breath of his mouth. . . . For he spake, and it was [done]; he commanded, and it stood fast. (Ps 33:6, 9)

> Let them praise the name of the LORD: for he commanded, and they were created. (Ps 148:5)

> And when he thus had spoken, he cried with a loud voice, Lazarus, come forth. (John 11:43)

Hence, God's word takes on the character of a living being, something "active," as Hebrews says. It "runs swiftly" in the world (Ps 147:15); it "melts" the snows (v. 18); it is "living" (*zoon*) and filled with "energy," or "active" like a two-edged sword, or discerning like eyes and understanding (Heb 4:12).

This must inform our understanding of Scriptural "fulfillment," which is probably not best seen as a subsequent "doing" of a cognitive "plan," but rather as the created form of the word's own being. God "fulfills" his word in the sense that the world temporally manifests what God does, manifests what the divine word *is*. The Hebrew or Greek terms are more suggestive than definitive: God "performs" his word (2 Chr 10:11); or he raises it up and carries it out (*quwm*, 1 Kgs 2:4), which has the sense of filling out in manifest form the divine reality already existent that is God's purpose. Hence, in the New Testamen, "fulfilling" a word, as in John 12:38 (*pleroo*), is similar to Hebrew words for "filling" up (*male*) that indicate creation itself. Solomon "fulfills" a word of the Lord concerning the house of Eli (1 Kgs 2:27) in the same sense that God blesses the animals at creation, and man and woman, and commands them to multiply and "fill" the earth (Gen 1:22, 28). God's word *is* that which creates the form of creaturely temporal being.

Here is where our own "natural" self-reflection and (speaking as a Christian) our faithful encounter with Scripture converge: if our histories are given by God, and if Scripture is the act of God's giving, then everything happens "according to the Scriptures," and Scripture constitutes and, in some divinely instrumental fashion, orders the shape of all our time. The conclusion to be drawn is important: it is not the case that Scripture "documents" the created world, such that there is a world in its historical forms that Scripture "documents," like a witness who gives a recorded statement of testimony with respect to this or that event. It is just the opposite: the world in its temporal appearance is a record of Scripture, that is, the created trace of God's own creating Word.

If and only if this is true, furthermore, it reconfigures how we should think of our own temporal existence, and its relation to Scripture. Our pasts, presents, and future—and these are deeply perplexing philosophical categories even if you are an atheist—find their real meaning solely as they are scripturally located. Past, present, and future are not about things that are lost forever, or about things that are yet to be created. Because they are located in the living Word of God, past, present, and future are "alive" to the purposes of God as Scripture speaks of them. Pascal's conversion, I believe, involved seeing that Abraham, Isaac, and Jacob, whose God is the "god of the living," constituted the shape of his life, the shape of his father's and mother's life, of France's life, of the church's. "Constitute": that is to say, all that Abraham and Isaac and Jacob are shown as doing and living, suffering and receiving, in the Scriptures was Pascal's own—it is ours. Pascal came to call these biblical persons (and other biblical elements) "figures," by which he meant that everything about their lives is made ours; for everything in the Scriptures is what the world *is*. We "figure" Scripture; and, ultimately, all that is in the Scriptures "figures" Christ, who is the Word himself in its perfected and uncreated being. In a real way, I *am*; as a creature I *am* Jacob—cheating, fleeing, fearful, trusting, patient, propagating, giving over. In a real way, as a set of creatures, the world *is* not only Genesis and Job, John and Revelation, but every word and passage in between. We don't need to *strive* to "follow Scripture"; we already are, by created definition. (Though our following may be Absalom's or Judah's, not David's or Peter's.) We need, rather, to take hold of this following, to give thanks for it, welcome it with joy—as Jesus says in the Parable of the Sower, to hear it, receive it, understand it, grow in it with patience (Mark 4:20; Matt 13:23; Luke 8:15). This is, of course, utterly transformative, in the sense that we now follow Scripture to its end.

II. SCRIPTURE AS TEMPORALITY'S TEMPLATE

1. God's Mind Is a Language

General audiences are familiar with the film *The Man Who Knew Infinity* (2015), about the brilliant Indian mathematician Srinivasa Ramanujan.[32] Ramanujan died at age thirty-two in 1920, having startled the world with unimagined insight into number theory. One of the key mysteries of Ramanujan's genius was how he "knew" what he knew. He would say things like "I just saw it," or that the formulae and so on came to him "in a dream" at night. It was a kind of visual epiphany. As a deeply religious—though not Christian—person, Ramanujan explained it all in terms of God: mathematical truths simply existed "in God." Famously, he said, "an equation has no meaning unless it expresses a thought of God."[33]

Scripture, I am arguing, is indeed God's "thought" "at work," as he creates the world. In general, the Christian tradition has until recently understood Scripture as somehow articulating the divine order of creation. Scripture, that is, is the expressive form of God's creative purpose. Through Scripture, or "according to it," God takes the abundance of his creatures, brings them into being, and gives them one to another. The full implications of this understanding were only rarely pressed explicitly, but again, traditionally Christians until recently intuited that the natural world, including human affairs themselves, is scripturally ordered and expresses these "thoughts of God" directly.

Obviously, this creates conceptual conundra. How can words scratched on a piece of paper, or printed in a book, be the causal form of the world, which is their expression? I doubt there is an easy solution to this problem. Anglicanism, in its sixteenth-century "Articles of Religion," referred to the Bible as "God's word written" (art. 20), which only gets at the issue, but at least lays it out clearly. By the sixteenth century, the question of religious authority had pitted "unwritten" tradition against the "written" Word of God; and although the argument was not in the first place metaphysical, it carried with it profound presuppositions, precisely because of the challenge involved in imagining specific linguistic signs as being God-derived, as opposed to following more fundamental pneumatic (and hence mysterious) promptings. John Wycliffe, two hundred years earlier, tried mightily, using sophisticated platonic philosophical frameworks, to trace the written word

---

32. The film was based on the book by Kanigel, *Man Who Knew Infinity*.
33. Ibid., 7, 67.

back up to the actual originating being of God, according to a ladder of metaphysical forms.[34]

In a way, this kind of puzzle was related to the search for an "original [human] language," answering the question of how human beings first began to speak. The first-century Jewish historian Josephus and others of his time had theorized an original "adamic" language, associated with the first man.[35] Augustine talked about it, and Origen before him alluded to it. Early Jewish writings were similarly interested in the question.[36] This idea was taken up in the Middle Ages. There was some debate over whether Hebrew was in fact that original language, although if not it was certainly close to it, or so many thought. By the Renaissance, this way of theorizing was set, and we can see it in the influential work of Johannes Reuchlin, which argued forcefully that the original language of humanity *was* Hebrew. Others, in Jewish and later Christian discussion in the seventeenth century, went on to claim that Hebrew itself *precedes* creation, and creation somehow is given out of or on the basis of the actual letters of Hebrew or primordial divine words that exist in God's mind, as it were. There is, so it was argued, such a thing as "God's language" in a literal sense. It's an old idea, but also an odd idea, although not as odd as moderns like to think. The sense that humans speak a language that is, as it were, on loan to them from God, and that language is not *only* human, hovers about the many attempts evolutionary linguists engage to parse a still strange etiology. From a Christian perspective, in any event, the working assumption has always been that the deepest link we have to God in our speaking is through the scriptural text itself. That, at least, is the logic at work in tying divine revelation to human speech itself. Hence, Christians in early modernity began to wonder more fundamentally about the way that sounds themselves are God-originated, and theories like Kepler's regarding the "music of the spheres" were, if not convincing, deeply compelling. This whole project of the seventeenth and eighteenth centuries needs to be revisited with a deeper theological awareness.

---

34. Levy, "John Wyclif's Neoplatonic View of Scripture."

35. See the essays in Coudert, ed., *Language of Adam*; and the introduction to Coudert's translation and edition of van Helmont's *Alphabet of Nature*. A rich discussion that identifies a range of theoretical currents is Bono, *Word of God and the Languages of Man*.

36. See Augustine's *City of God* 16:11; perhaps Origen, *Contra Celsum* 5:30 (a "divine" language"); and likewise the Babylonian Talmud (J. Megillah 1:11) as "God's language."

Wycliffe's metaphysical analysis of the Bible was really an attempt to understand Scripture on its own terms.[37] He argued that God's own counsel or interior Word (see below) is that which the Bible, as a material object of letters and words, presents. Scripture, in its written or spoken and heard verbal forms—its "words"—is, as it were, a created function of the counsel of God, as these divine thoughts are temporally presented and received by human beings. More than that, however, Scripture is therefore a function of that which orders temporarily itself: it is the way time *making* appears in time. Scripture presents to us how our times are ordered. We can now engage this idea, already presented, on the basis of Scripture itself.

A key intrascriptural claim is that God has a "counsel," an interior purpose to his being. Isaiah 14 (vv. 24-27) speaks to this directly and classically: "The LORD of hosts hath sworn, saying, Surely as I have thought, so shall it come to pass; and as I have purposed, [so] shall it stand: That I will break the Assyrian in my land, and upon my mountains tread him under foot . . . This [is] the purpose that is purposed upon the whole earth: and this [is] the hand that is stretched out upon all the nations. For the LORD of hosts hath purposed, and who shall disannul [it]? and his hand [is] stretched out, and who shall turn it back?" God's purpose is his act. In Isaiah 9:6 that purpose is given in the Messiah's own active form: "mighty counsellor" or "purpose."

Hence, Job (23:13-14) writes that "he [is] in one [mind], and who can turn him? and [what] his soul desireth, even [that] he doeth. For he performeth [the thing that is] appointed for me: and many such [things are] with him." And the psalmist (33:11) proclaims that "The counsel of the LORD standeth for ever, the thoughts of his heart to all generations."

Shall we then say that God has a "mind"? The New Testament uses the term (Rom 8:27; 1 Cor 2:16) for God and Christ, while in the Old Testament the word sometimes translated as "mind" is really that for a voice (*peh*) or spirit (*nephesh*) or heart (*leb*). This fluidity of referents is itself significant: the mind of God is given—in the sense of being able to be identified, or manifest for what it is—in its articulate expression; and that expression is given in God's performance or act. That is, God's counsel or mind *is* God's word. To speak of God thinking or planning or willing or construing is to

---

37. Levy, "John Wyclif's Neoplatonic View of Scripture." See also the discussion of Wycliffe and his contemporaries—closer to him in many fundamental ways than later Protestants understood—in Levy, *Holy Scripture and the Quest for Authority*. For accessible introductions to Jewish interpretation, see the sections on creation in Kugel, *Traditions of the Bible*, 44-91.

posit a divine "word" or words. We could point to a long list of examples, where "word" is not just a covenant (Heb 6:17) but underlies the whole of creation, on the one hand, because it is the very act of God's purposive being, on the other. God's word "lasts forever" (Isa 40:8); it accomplishes its purpose and is never empty (Isa 55:11); it is "settled in heaven" (Ps 119:89).

When Scripture therefore speaks of something happening "according to his word," this "according to" is not simple: it represents an encompassing realty of foundation and agency given in the Word of God, rather than simply an external plan: God speaks of "in my word" and "by my word," and so on (Num 3:16, 51; 4:45; 14:20; 36:5). The great culmination of this kind of phraseology comes in Psalm 119 (vv. 9, 25, 28, 41). One is cleansed by heeding God's word, quickened by that word, strengthened by it, granted mercy and salvation in it, blessed by it, made wise in it, delivered through it (Ps 119:58, 65, 76, 107, 154, 169–71).

2. God's Language as Creative

Genesis, as a creation account and taken as a whole, is the articulation of divine "word establishment": God speaks creation, but that speaking also takes form in the words that are then articulated in the ordinances of Moses, the Prophets, and Psalms. Jesus, in Luke 24, in speaking of the "scriptures" that speak of him, is also immediately (in the canonical ordering of the Gospels) identified as the speaker in John 1. These are made the words of "life" itself, which are themselves life-"giving."

Jewish tradition, as in the Genesis Rabbah (1.1), came to view specific words of Scripture as preceding and ordering Scripture, linking the Torah to the Wisdom of Proverbs 8.[38] Some Christians took this up themselves. God "looks into" the Torah as he creates. But this is because the Torah is God's own "counsel" or "mind," not an "external" set of letters that somehow God takes hold of and then applies as a tool. From and in this Word, God does what God wills. The image of God's "book" then emerges, as in the Psalms—a term that refers to writing letters and words in a given document. "Then said I, Lo, I come: in the volume of the book [it is] written of me" (Ps 40:7). The psalmist's tears are "in [God's] book" (56:8), as is each limb of a created foetus listed therein (139:16), even as the wicked are "blotted" from "the book of the living" (69:28). Revelation, as we know, brings the notion of God's "book" to a high pitch, referring to it twenty-three

---

38. See Boyarin, "Gospel of the Memra."

Preface: Natural Theology and the Bible

times, ending with the final establishment of the New Jerusalem and its members as being "written in the Lamb's book of life" (Rev 21:27, RSV).

The notion that created life is given in a divine "book" is of course something that could be taken strictly as a similitude or imaginative metaphor. My aim is not to do away with the concept of metaphor here, but to locate its originating force: we have books that we can touch and read, that have pages and letters, *only because* there is such a thing as a "book" of God. Human books are, in the platonic scheme, reflections of the archetypal "book"; *they* are the "metaphors" of something more substantive. It is *not* that we know what human books are and from this we project book-like analogies onto divine realities. The issue is not, in any case, Platonism. It is, rather, a question of divine creative precedence: we have human books because God creatively made this possible, not only in ordering the parameters of possibility, but in founding the being of each and every created "thing" by which books exist at all. All human speech is metaphorical in the sense that it is dependent upon divine reality and initiative.

Indeed, the notion of a divine book is not just one among many; it is foundational itself. "The Word written," in the Anglican phraseology, links human writing to a divine Word that is on its own terms primordial, because it is God himself. There are human books, because there is a Word that is God's own being, and that being is Word because that is simply who God is. Words do not exist apart from this one Word who is God. The human being as "image" of God, then, is a word-using creature, whose own artifacts, verbally as much as anything, are given according to God's own use in a primary way. God's book precedes all other books.

So too, then, does the "naming" of the world by human beings reflect the naming of all things by God. Religious philosophers have long reflected on the nature of human "analogy" in speaking about God. Thomas Aquinas was one of the richest writers on the topic.[39] The basic idea is that human beings can never either conceive of God or speak of God in a sufficient way as to "know" or describe God in an exact way. God cannot be contained by human ideas or terms. Nonetheless, these human categories are properly used by what we call "analogy." When we call God "wise," what are referring to? We know "wisdom" (perhaps!) in a human context, but how apply that term to God? We do so, Aquinas and others argued, by "analogy," knowing that in some way what we know about our own human wisdom does indeed apply to God in a meaningful way. The philosophic intricacies of

---

39. The most famous texts are from Thomas' *Summa Theologiae* 1a. q. 13.

how this is so need not concern us here. They are difficult to follow.⁴⁰ But I would underline a key element of Aquinas's discussion of analogy, at least with respect to terms we use for God: causality. God "causes" our lives, our beings and doings, in a fundamental way. He is our creator at the deepest level. Thus, even our linguistic terms and references derive from the creative act of God. We can call God "wise" because God has created the very concept and its linguistic term to be used by human beings to refer to him. We can probably go further and say that God has caused this term's use and reference insofar as it somehow reflects the truth of who God is. That is—and this is perhaps a Thomistic claim—there is an ontological link between our language for God, in this case, and God himself.

What exactly that link may be is perhaps not crucial to sort out. What we *can* say is that the link—not just its authorization, but its very form—is given in Scripture. Scripture calls God "wise": "Now unto the King eternal, immortal, invisible, the only wise God, [be] honour and glory for ever and ever. Amen" (1 Tim 1:17). Not only is this the ground for our calling God "wise," but it is the ground for the truth of our so speaking of God. Scripture embodies the ontological link between our apprehension and communication—our experience—of God and God himself.

If this is true, as I believe it is, then the whole of history—the created reality that is given by God—is thus scripturally grounded. Everything that time offers us is "first" given in Scripture. From this reality, furthermore, it is appropriate to speak of the scriptural encyclopedia of nature itself—which brings us back to the traditional Christian claim about the "two books," now properly ordered. While the natural world can be looked at on many levels, including empirical or theoretical scientific categories, these elements themselves, in all their particularity, can be apprehended and articulated in human thought and speech because they are "given" first in Scripture, the analogically causative form of God's primary creative action. This could include both the strange and the familiar creatures of the Bible, from the coney and gazelle to leviathan and behemoth. The actual translation issues here are significant: we don't know, often, what species of animal or plant in our own experience an ancient Hebrew word may be referring to. But just because of this the Hebrew words provoke us: the fact that they *do* refer to living things whose depth of identity—miracles of presence in a world that grants them space and name, that *is* simply that

---

40. Mondin, *Principle of Analogy*; McInerny, *Aquinas and Analogy*; and, from an evangelical perspective, Spencer, *Analogy of Faith*.

Preface: Natural Theology and the Bible

divine grant—demands that we engage in a practice of word rummaging, mining, and scraping.

3. The Natural Forms of Scripture's Creative Wisdom

We can take as an example the animal that the Authorized Version translates as "coney" the *shaphan* of Psalm 104:8; Proverbs 30:26; and Leviticus 11:5. When it comes to the modern referent of this animal, the Greeks translated it as "porcupine" (*cherogrillus*), and Christian writers like Jerome pressed this into the form of the hedgehog, or "irchin" (*ericius*). The English translators, from Wycliffe to Coverdale, used the term "coney," meaning "rabbit" in our modern usage; but "coney" itself came to slip into significations like "rock badger" and "marmot." Today, scholars view the *shaphan* as referring to the animal known as the hyrax (of which at least four species are known), small herbivorous mammals closely related biologically to the elephant, of all things—not a rodent at all. So what is Scripture actually talking about, actually "creating," as it were, in the world we live in when it speaks of the *shaphan*?

Jerome, taking up a range of biblical animals, understands these beasts, just in their scriptural verbal location, as cracking open the avenues of moral struggle and destiny before God. These taxonomic referential explorations, however, are only a part of the naturalistic lexicon of the Scriptures. "The mountains are the right habitat for the slayer of the wise serpent"—the serpent that, in the garden of paradise, was wiser than all the beasts, the serpent that deceived Eve. "The cliffs are a refuge for rock badgers" (Ps 104:18, NKJV). "He who is fearful has a rock-fastness for his refuge; the rock, moreover, is Christ."[41] The *shaphan*, then, speaks of the Christian who relies on Christ in the face of Satan. Augustine makes a similar claim, stressing the spines of the hedgehog, which point to human sins, and overall to our wretchedness, while the hedgehog nonetheless can take refuge in the high rocks, which are Christ's.[42] The psalm itself, in Jerome's reading, opens up to view an arena of God's "works," even while it indicates the way that Christ's followers are "filled" by the blessings that correspond to these works. To be sure, you have to work hard to get such a meaning from the "coney."

The early nineteenth-century poet John Banton, much reviled by his better, John Clare, was doing no different than Jerome when he devoted

41. Homily 30, in Jerome, *Homilies*, 226.
42. Exposition 3 of Ps 103, in Augustine, *Expositions of the Psalms 99–120*, 159.

a complete song to "The Conies" in his popular collection *Gleanings in Carmel*: "The Conies of the mountains are a frail and feeble race; 'This is the generation, Lord, of them that seek they face;' Not many noble, rich or great, compose that little flock, Who have their habitations in the all-sufficient Rock."[43] There was nothing provocative here, to be sure, but the long poem rehearses a deeply "probative" devotion that is meant to use Scripture to uncover the pathway towards mortality's transfiguration in the forms of the natural world. Clare himself would turn to the coney as a sign of female promiscuity,[44] just as others would later exegete its scriptural human nomenclature (as in Ezek 8:11) in terms of totemistic animal idolatry, which had penetrated into the inner precincts of Israel's religious leadership.[45]

This kind of word rummaging is obviously not a scientific enterprise but a literary one, bound to the peculiar literary object that is the Bible (as well as to the concerns, often culturally and psychologically ordered, of the rummagers). It is literary in that it is about scriptural words. But the words do not, as it were, stick to the page, but are pursued as they leap off into a world constantly recreated before our eyes as the context of our lives. Rather than fancy at work, there is a simple but fundamental metaphysical conviction, suggested by the eighteenth-century Anglican philosopher Joseph Butler's notion of Scripture as an "abridgement of the history of the world."[46] Butler insisted on the analogy of the scriptural world to the natural world—not on the basis of "kind," but finally on the basis of their intersecting structure vis-à-vis God: Scripture and nature engage us in the "same" reality of life, which *is* God, the God who forms all of our own created experiential world.

Yet Scripture is also different from nature, in that its form, from a human perspective, is purer in its signifying virtues, such that our natural lives and their form help us to be open to Scripture's way of talking. But Scripture itself actually proves to explain how this works more clearly, and more fundamentally. Scriptural structures of reality seep into our natural perceptions—our relationships with the natural world—and show them for what they are, even if, from an experiential point of view, we draw our

43. Banton, *Gleanings in Carmel*, 16.
44. On Clare vs. Banton, see Bate, *John Clare*, 546; on Clare's use of the "coney," see 459.
45. Jacobs, "Are There Totem-Clans in the Old Testament?," 158.
46. Butler, *Analogy of Religion*, 259.

initial sense about these structures from nature itself. Only then are we opened to grasping how Scripture's ordering truths work.

We can take an example that moves from the coney to the natural world of human fabrication: the iPhone. We know that the iPhone's use is now ubiquitous. Many of us find it annoying to go to a restaurant and have one's friends pull out their phones; constant iPhone use can even be dangerous for pedestrians crossing a busy street. Some psychologists speak of "addiction," in precise cognitive-chemical terms, with respect to iPhone use.[47] But it is also possible—and surely morally required—to hazard a specifically *scriptural* judgment about iPhones, if indeed their placement in our world is tied to a world that comes to us from God. In this case, we might well say that the iPhone is a *figure* of distraction, which tumbles out of a scriptural study of a host of different scriptural persons.

If we want to deal with the topic of "distraction," there are some obvious places in Scripture to go: "But the cares of the world, and the delight in riches, and the desire for other things, enter in and choke the word, and it proves unfruitful" (Mark 4:19, RSV). "Cares" here, *merimna*, literally refers to being drawn away, distracted. Fair enough. Thus, "the Lord answered her, 'Martha, Martha, you are anxious [from *merimna*] and troubled about many things'" (Luke 10:41, RSV). So we can observe that "listening," hearkening, being attentive, hearing, works against distraction. There are a host of words and contexts, from Deuteronomy to the Psalms to Isaiah to Job to Jeremiah, and of course Jesus himself, that speak to this theme. One can then develop moral exhortations on the basis of this—I have seen these in various Bible study outlines. These scriptural verses could provide us with advice in the form of a proverb: "Let thine eyes look right on, and let thine eyelids look straight before thee" (Prov 4:25).

This kind of scriptural thematic approach to "distraction" is good. But the question is: what *is* the iPhone in or "according to" God's creative Word? Figures of "distraction" abound in the Scriptures. Is the iPhone a figure of the Egyptian sorcerer's rod? The gold of Elijah's servant? The dishes of Martha? The oxen of the wedding invitee who will not go to the feast? It is worth asking that because of course to enter into an answer is to discover who one is oneself . . . and what God is actually doing to you and to your world . . . and to ours. Here we rise from the level of personal decision—how I shall order my day, what my personal disciplines are for the use of my technology—to something far greater: the shape of history.

47. Achenbach, "Teen Confronts Her iPhone Addiction."

Perhaps the iPhone is found amid the accoutrements of Babylon and the empires (Jas 4:13; Rev 18:17, etc.), whose merchants, in their enslavement to their goods, wail at the ruin of their consuming possessions in the face of God. Thus, it is probably very much the case that the iPhone is found in Scripture, lodged among the ensnaring attractions of Egypt or Rome, Israel, or Galilee, just as much as our individual sins are lodged in the hairs of the coney. We can "find ourselves" there, with a shudder of recognition:

> But they all alike began to make excuses. The first said to him, "I have bought a field, and I must go out and see it; I pray you, have me excused." And another said, "I have bought five yoke of oxen, and I go to examine them; I pray you, have me excused." And another said, "I have married a wife, and therefore I cannot come" (Luke 14:18–20, RSV). But take heed to yourselves lest your hearts be weighed down with dissipation and drunkenness and cares of this life, and that day come upon you suddenly like a snare (Luke 21:34, RSV). For Demas, in love with this present world, has deserted me and gone to Thessalonica; Crescens has gone to Galatia, Titus to Dalmatia. (2 Tim 4:10, RSV)

The logical priority of Scripture is important in all theologians of analogy of this sort. It is explained in various ways. But the priority itself is important to grasp. If God has a "mind," a counsel of his own self, then Scripture is properly speaking the "mind of God." *Logoi* and *rhemata* in the New Testament refer to vocalized words spoken. Jesus himself uses them as synonyms for the divine Word vocalized by the prophets and given in written Scripture (John 10:25) by Jesus himself (John 14:23) and by the apostolic witness (hence the written words of what will become the articulated gospel of the New Testament—John 17:8, 14, 20). For Jesus, the Word incarnate, to say that "my words [*rhemata*] are life" (John 6:63) is, on the basis of the analogy, something other than a linguistic metaphor. It is, rather, an ontological revelation: when I speak, the world's shape comes to be, in "weal and woe" both, as God says in Isaiah 45:7 (RSV), "peace and evil" (AV).

4. The Vocation of Our Temporal Existence

What are we meant to do as human beings? Temporal being, from a moral standpoint, is all about searching after, discerning, and embracing the purposes of divine grace in the existence of all things. Our lives are in part themselves a vocation to search for this connection.

Preface: Natural Theology and the Bible

When Jesus asserts that his "words are spirit and life" in John 6:63, it is in the midst of an encounter regarding his incarnate being and how human beings can somehow engage it. The discussion gives rise—especially as it touches on the ingestion of his body and blood—to a parting of the ways with many erstwhile disciples. They have been struggling, perhaps for too long, with who their master really is, and how they might follow him. "Many therefore of his disciples, when they had heard [this], said, This is an hard saying; who can hear it?" (John 6:60). The *logos* of Jesus, both in its specific focus on eating his flesh and drinking his blood, as well as its entire presentation within the synagogue, strikes against his listeners' consciousness as an "unyielding" object. Unable to take hold of it—they have no power to hear it or obey it—they give up. Jesus knows they will not "believe," and indeed they leave him. Then Jesus turns to the Twelve and asks if they too will go away. "Then Simon Peter answered him, Lord, to whom shall we go? thou hast the words [*rhemata*] of eternal life" (John 6:68).

To follow Jesus is to wrestle with his words, and finally to become people where his word(s) "abide" (e.g., John 15:7). The claim and invitation is founded not on some late-coming christological construction of truth, but on the basic order of the Torah: "And these words, which I command thee this day, shall be in thine heart" (Deut 6:6). It is an order then insinuated into the devotional sinews of Israel (cf. Ps 119:11), which becomes the active exercise of faithfulness. Hence, "searching" the Scriptures (John 5:39; Acts 17:11), both in Jesus's and the apostolic contexts, stands not simply for the task of truth discovery, but for a way of life bound to grace (such as Jesus indicates at the end of John 6). The encounter with the living Jesus among the confused disciples on the way to Emmaus is one of scriptural unfolding (Luke 24:27; cf. 24:7–8): they are led to see that what has "happened," including their own lives, is a part of Scripture itself. Wrestling with the words of the Word, with Scripture, unveils their creative reach, and hence the truth of who we are.

It is worth repeating a major claim that I am making that undergirds the possibility of a natural theology. It isn't the case simply that "our times"—our lives and the happenings that constitute our lives—are "like" the times of Scripture. We do not, in any case, really know what Scripture's "time" or "history" is like: for Scripture is God's creative spring for all times and histories.

This claim obviously goes against the grain of most historical approaches to the study of the world, which in their scientific methodology presuppose a uniform time that exclusively applies to all events under examination. There is, however, little reason to think that time in Scripture is fundamentally like our experience at all. The diversity of scriptural interpretive moves indicates the impossibility of defining in advance the nature of the biblical narrative's temporal "duration," that is, what constitutes its "diachronic" character and the temporal flow of its discourse. We can take the book of Proverbs, which we like to see as good, even truly founded, advice, as an example: from a modern critical perspective, the book of Proverbs is a collection of adages, including within themselves compilations from different sources (Lemuel, etc.?); it also includes theological discourses (ch. 8) that take on the voices of literary personifications of abstract categories ("Wisdom"). The proverbs themselves—"A slothful man will not catch his prey, but the diligent man will get precious wealth" (Prov 12:27, RSV)—are meant to be expositions of permanent (what exactly does this mean?) truths gleaned perhaps from someone's (whose?) personal experience and observation; there are in fact personal names that appear, indicating "historical" personages. This critical parsing uncovers within the text a diversity of literary genres. These can be identified, with some dispute, and their originating and then editorial contexts articulated, again with some dispute. All this constitutes normal historical criticism.

What becomes difficult to identify, however, is the temporal character both behind and expressed in the book of Proverbs. Historical critics can claim to maintain a single temporal discourse in their discussions of origins, assigning possible dates and contexts to this or that part of the text. But this critical discourse cannot include the temporal modalities of the proverbs themselves—their "permanent" truths—nor can it identify the temporal status of the named compilers in their textual presence (Solomon, Agur, Lemuel). Such critical discourse cannot, furthermore, engage the theological claims to divine creation that are made in (e.g.) chapter 8, or the natural repetitions of some of the creatures—the ants, for instance, or the locusts and lizard (ch. 30)—in their demonstration of wisdom. What is the "history" that the *book* itself presents? The temporal planes that the historical critic can try to identify in the book obviously intersect, but not in a way that the book itself (or other biblical books that engage Proverbs) can resolve, let alone explain. They exist—Lemuel, agricultural peoples, Egyptian wisdom texts, Israelite scribal editing—in a single container that is all.

Preface: Natural Theology and the Bible

What is the "time" of the book of Proverbs that ours is "like"? In this case, as in all others with respect to Scripture, the Bible's time comes to us diversely, with respect to our own experience. That the Bible has a "time" that can be related to ours at all is given as a divine claim that defies any integrating human apprehension. The Bible's time is utterly asymmetrical by analogy to our own. Instead of helpfully illuminating our temporal experience, the Bible's time questions and uncovers human ignorance. Thus, we must *search*. Scriptural scrutiny is a moral imperative—and natural theology is a form of this vocation or *examen*.

5. Reading Scripture Is a Way of Doing Natural Theology

Here we can return to Pascal's (and the Gospels') Jesus, who speaks of the "God of the living" (Mark 12:27), that is, of Abraham and Isaac and Jacob, who *are* alive. Let us place these words in the context of mortal human relations, which, after all, was the topic Jesus himself was engaging within the context of these words in his discussion with the Sadducees. A woman's husband dies, she then is married to a series of now-dead husband's brothers, and one by one they all die. Whose wife is she at the resurrection? Let us acknowledge that this is a real experience for most people at some point: a dead spouse, a dead child, a dead sibling or friend—for most people all these often within the space of a short span of experience. "Whose" are you? Some of us have known families in Africa who have lost mother, brother, daughter, and uncle to AIDS within just a few months. Or we could note the phenomenon of war, which can do the same thing in a day, an hour, a minute. We are taught in our Western cultures that these people are "just dead," on the one hand; religiously, then, we hope for resolutions according to our faith, whatever it is. But everybody knows that this is not how it works, psychologically anyway. Whatever one's faith or lack of it, one ruminates over those who have died: over stories, encounters, and outcomes. Why did this happen the way it did? How could I have done something differently? What do I remember of this or that conversation? He told me this; she did that on our trip; we saw such and such together; I remember praying with him about that. As we do this, we come over time to certain resolutions of faith, or perhaps dead ends of sorrow.

This is what happens in the "natural world," with our memories bound up with the often untidy pile of our lived relationships. I make the analogy of such a sifting and encountering and restructuring with our reading of Scripture; but in this case it is Scripture itself that is constantly taking hold of these very relationships, given in memory and encounter, and reordering them for us. It is as if Scripture were our own consciousness—which it is, in a sense, by grace. To draw on personal experience, I can point to my immediate family's difficult experience of suicide, which has destroyed the life of a mother and sister. At a certain point, when I came to faith and began reading the Bible, I would search for clarity about some of this Scripture, in a straightforward way: what does the Bible "say" about suicide? This is a standard and to some extent helpful approach that treats Scripture as a kind of guidebook to natural problems. Within the Bible, thus, one can find a few examples of suicide—Samson, Saul, Paul wishing he could die (maybe)—and from these one can try to learn "what the Bible says about suicide." If one were more intellectually adventurous, one then would move into a similar examination of the early church's discussion. It is all as if one were putting together an ethical handbook: here are your examples; here are the arguments; here are the conclusions; here are the rules. It is a necessary task.

In the end, however, it is not what most of us actually do in reading Scripture as a discipline. Rather, in reading Scripture it is not just who is right and who is wrong, or what action is to be approved and what avoided that comes up. Rather, in reading Scripture we discover *who* people are. Samson's desperation, and disappointment, then energized by a kind of hope bound to destruction. Saul's self-hatred and final fears and anguish; but also Saul's uncovering, in the midst of this, a world of hovering spirits—like the dead Samuel, who will speak to him. Samson returns in the great list of the faithful in Hebrews 11, of those who await the new life given by Christ to his followers. But Saul himself disappears completely from the Bible after his death, except in the sorrowing song of David, where he applies to Saul words involving beauty, glory, and love that are even sometimes applied to God (2 Sam 1:17–27). Unless, of course, we count the violent passions of another Saul—a "blasphemer," "persecutor," "insulter," worthy of nothing but wrath, yet who was showered with divine grace (1 Tim 1:13–4)—unless we count *that* Saul as a figure joined to his namesake. If one traverses that scriptural landscape back and forth over time, one will likely see that God has been doing something with the very people—in this case, the dead—that one had not before recognized.

The reader of Scripture, reading in this way by which Scripture is allowed to disclose the natural world's felt contours according to its own internal meaning, discovers divine creation at work. In doing this, the reader is changed. And while it is a traditional claim that reading Scripture changes us, the implication goes further: reading Scripture changes the world of our experience; it changes how the pieces are actually put together, what their "real" history in God's hands is. Reading Scripture actually *changes the world* as it stands to us. Forgiveness, hope, compassion, and strength, among other realities of our relatedness to the world, could come to be only because God is indeed "the God of living"—not simply teaching lessons through Scripture, but creatively forming life through them. Time is utterly malleable in God's hands.

Reading Scripture, in a way that has been fairly unremarkable yet consistent over the centuries, opens one up to the nature of the times in which we live, and in which the world comes to us—which is another way of speaking of "time"—as a gift from God.

What does it mean for things to "happen"? When we experience things as "happening," we apprehend their place within God's ordering purpose; we notice God's use of his creation, its givenness from his hand. What does it mean for things to happen? It means that the world is "according to Scripture," God's very Word, which precedes all things.

6. Natural Theology as Poetry

Everything is something else, even as it remains what it is. Time, as God uses it, is built on this reality. Ultimately, we can find its truth, its "everything," in the Scriptures. But because this ultimate frame is not a code to be deciphered, but rather the road of that endless but abundant movement that is divine grace given to the creature, we can leave these bits of "what it is" to their wandering under the sky of the Word.

Poems do this better than most other ways of knowing or apprehending; that is, they do this willingly. Poems do this in the sense that, in their formal discreteness and descriptive isolation, they let our times shift, shimmer, and disappear, only to become other times or kinds of time as they also offer allusive associations.[48] From a Christian perspective, this process of temporal shifting can be poetically instanced through descriptive discourse because time itself is just this set of experienced displacements

---

48. Description, even if understood in some basic mimetic way, is neither uniform in its act and consequence nor simple. Nonetheless, descriptive poetry *is* a distinct enterprise and stands against other theories of poetic purpose, largely because, with whatever anxieties and scepticism, it posits an actual "world" that one encounters to which one is discursively responsible. See the opening chapter and then various studies in Spiegelman, *How Poets See the World*.

that derive from God's purpose, which is given "according to Scripture." Yet this happening is independent of our apprehensions themselves. Hence, "Christian poetry" in this sense is less *about* God in Christ than it is an enacted willingness for God to allow his times to be encountered and received, under whatever rubric. And the natural theology that is bound to poetry is simply the practiced "yes" behind this will.

The poems that make up the rest of this volume are, then, simply a form of practice.

They are are written by a theologian, not by a poet of means. There are, to be sure, remarkable religious poets whose writings are theologically profound, from St. Ephrem to Christina Rossetti. Religious poets like these demand their own treatment, and have righty received it, as much for their formal virtues as for the character of the things about which they write. Theologians who write poetry are different. They too exist in a long tradition, from Gregory of Nazianzus to Isaac Williams and beyond (and of varying quality). But poetry, for them, is only one means of getting theologically at certain truths that are rightly given in this form. In the present case, the point, in part, is to offer a discrete referent within the created world whose form can be specifically limned in a limited context—a lived context, we might say—but whose reality is then allowed to begin the process of multiple reflection within the world of God's infinite creative purpose. This is ultimately, as I have argued, a scriptural explication that is pursued through the encounter of lived forms and scriptural forms themselves.

As a form of natural theology, theological poetry constitutes the search for scriptural order in the world of things, which itself represents God's use of creation. This is hardly a ruled discipline, for although scriptural form is determinate, it is also infinitely referring and ordering itself. From this comes the "rummaging" character of the process. The theologian or reader constantly returns to the discrete natural referents of the poem and begins the trek outwards anew; here are circling backs, restings in place, abrupt leaps across lines of reference. In particular, the process opens up the temporal sphere of reference, so that the natural artifacts in play—be they persons, beasts, plants, events, memories—can loosen historical chronology for the sake of scriptural form's disclosure. None of this happens in set sequence, nor does it happen within any single reading of a poem itself; that is, divine usage—the basis of "time"—is not so much embedded in things as displayed in their encounter with other things, God himself in the end. Hence, the natural world always remains what it is in

Preface: Natural Theology and the Bible

any encounter, including the most constrained of temporal experiences, which is that of mortality. Just this constraint is often the last word of any theological description of the natural world, at least outside its divine redemptive consummation. Unlike other forms of theology, natural theology often finds its ultimate articulation in simple descriptive strokes, a setting forth and a letting go.

The character of the poems that follow engage this process, sometimes moving directly to the revealed scriptural character of things, but even more so leaving things hanging in that space where time, or divine usage, is left unfinished and unpredicted and where, at best, Scripture emerges or takes hold only allusively. There are lots of animals, plants, and rocks in these poems, as one might expect if the natural world means anything; just as there are marriages, children, births, and deaths. Inevitably, these elements are refracted in a personal way, something that is also intrinsic to our created condition and hence intrinsic to the object of natural theology. The aspects of the natural world the poems present could be categorized, in part, in this way:

i. Ordering of birth and death

- The miraculous limits to our being; breath; the arc of life

ii. Ordering of transient encounter

- Providence, but also ethics

iii. Figural order

- Absorption of world by the Word—God's shaping of life in Scripture

iv. Exhaustion and despair of finding

- Temporal order is crushing in part because of our ignorance in knowing Scripture and receiving it in the world (one thinks of Hardy's "The Sigh"). This is as it should be: we turn to the Lord to be saved.

v. Sin and its overcoming in the midst of the scriptural figure: time as change

- Salvation as the reordering of our limited discernments and failures. This is apprehended in terms of moments, changes, coming to be—the shadow of our very creation.

vi. Living past

- Our reception of all God's gifts lies in our entrance into the one company of the saints.

Each of the following poems is given a temporal title, one that reflects the artifact described but also implies its nature as a thing that is divinely useful, and in fact used in different ways by human creatures and ultimately, in hope, by God. Rocks, for instance, have a range of times that reflect these usages and are, from any theological perspective, at best simply laid out, as on a table, before the choices of their maker. So too for all the elements of the world, from drunkenness to marriage, from stars and insects to the wars of the tropics. All these elements are finally placed, in accordance with any theological reflection upon the natural world, together within the shadow of God's own pressuring form, scripturally allusive or sometimes explicitly stated, in this collection within a closing set of encounters with Lent and Easter, whose reality dictates the range of the world's times in various ways. There is no other special order to their presentation, besides the alphabet, which is all that nature requires. In a future volume, I will lay out more carefully the boundaries within which scriptural revelation takes hold of these natural forms in a comprehensive fashion. But here the purpose is quite modestly to open doors, not trace out the cartographic lines of the Word's globe.

Good descriptive poetry, from John Clare to Mary Oliver, does not require a scriptural grid to disclose God's shadow on the world. But for this shadow to become an animating spirit, of faith or hope or love, the scriptural origins of that world a poet may name require a certain scrutiny, immersive and exploratory. Much of this is rightly oblique, for the sake of the exploration itself, which must lead us literally everywhere, a place which alone is God's.

POEMS

ACROSTIC TIME

All things happen after three days.
Before that, the sum of them is in one place,
calmly or angrily, sleeping or singing a song.
Dawn to dusk, dawn to dusk, dawn:
everything transpires now, the days multiplied.
Forests spill across the planets' sides,
grass springs up in the cracks of things;
heavens wrap themselves in layers and rings,
ice covers the globes, then breaks and runs.
Juice drips in pools from warm plums.
Kelp ties up the fish into glistening knots.
Letters tumble about, shouted or thought.
Mosquitoes sneak into houses spitting blood.
Nasturtiums mix their reds and oranges with the mud.
Otters, beavers, seals lose their skins.
Promises, avowals, scoffing, growls and grins
quiver as the ground quakes and careens.
Rust streaks the rocks and covers the machines.
Saturn remains unknown but always glows.
Tabitha stands, the darkness trembling and slowing.
Unseen wings flutter furiously in the hills.
Vast containers continue to be filled,
waste, like water, rushes in rivers of pity,
xenotic flesh slips its grave outside the city,
young and old among them, ugly, pretty.
Zero, one, zero one, counting
off to infinity.

ACCOUNTING TIME

The rooster is the most alert of beasts.
He keeps night vigils in the heat and cold.
He never rests, while lords sit at their feasts.

Luca Pacioli, artisan of spheres and priest
of profits, taught us how we gain our gold:
the rooster is the most alert of beasts.

Take note, therefore, of how your sums increase,
of what you lose, of what you've bought and sold:
and never rest while lords sit at their feasts!

However great it is, even the least,
line each of them in columns, for behold,
the rooster is the most alert of beasts:

he watches what has risen, fallen, ceased,
the hopes that soar or crash as heaven foretold;
he never rests while lords sit at their feasts

and, drinking, kick the dog in a caprice
of song by which the round earth is consoled . . .
the rooster, too, the most alert of beasts.

But who would build the rooster's house or piece
by piece restore its limbs when it grows old?
How can it rest while lords eat at their feasts?

For vain it is to rise when pans are greased
with oil and wine poured in the stewing bowl.
The rooster is the most alert of beasts
who rests now that his Lord decides to feast.

ADULT TIME

I.

You're entering a world where there's only advice,
where command and subservience are no longer;
where you're expected to be wise
or something stronger.

They put your suggestions in a bowl,
then, with everyone else's, shake them together
and, mixing in silver and gold,
they divine the weather.

At first there's pleasure in matching the two,
calculating outcomes from the algebra of many hearts.
Then the clouds obscure the view,
the dew departs,

storm winds and drought arise.
"I told you so," or something like that, you'll say.
Then you'll clutch your sides
and pray.

I suppose it makes no difference that you're older:
in this sense, you'll still be crying out for aid,
as the days grow colder and colder
and the light turns grey.

What then is wisdom all about?
Or that stronger thing I mentioned? It's not what they say:
not thought in a bowl. It's crying out:
everywhere, always.

Chasing the Shadow

II.

There's another thing to say to you,
since I know that all the stuff above seems bleak:
the patch of sky that's blue
has everything you seek

if you go deep inside of it—
colors, luxuriance, running, shouts.
Even when the clouds drip,
more blue pours out.

This earth, alone in all of space
where millions of hush-stilled worlds wonder as they see
all things mirrored in its face,
as they were and will be.

So you're where you should be; and it's clear
you'd be foolish if you wanted another place or time.
Crying out just here
is wrapped in the sublime.

ANNIVERSARY TIME

Francis Mercury van Helmont
poured over his Paracelsan texts
and Kabbalah, then fell on
the key to "twenty-six"'s blessed
treasures of hope:

its tangents hide inside
their slopes "Yahweh" himself, creating
worlds of vast and wide
excesses, stars and the fates
and fires they stoke.

Five plus six plus five
plus ten, the gematrist has pointed
to this year as dust enlivened
in the furnace of anointing
Spirit's breath.

Or is this rather just the list
of Asher's generations sent
off into exile's mists?
Or Benjamin's rosy-cheeked young men
assembled for death?

Scripture! ripped from the spheres
or the moon's last epicycled run,
we wander instead into a year
like a field's far corner, scattered with the sun's
droppings and forgettings,

the small trees and stones,
some new grass and barren holes
bottomed by eyes, glowing . . .
what an empty sky! unfolded
on our settlings and begetting!

2016—having fled Lebanon in 1990

Chasing the Shadow

BAKING TIME

I buried some leavened dough
in the corner of the yard last month, just where
the fence has listed away, and the tears
in the hedge are wide. They had stowed

an old barrel there
years before, maybe for the rain
from the neighbors' now rotting garage, stained
by age, barely carrying

the slope of its roof. It was a peace-
offering to the worms. We had taken away
the barrel, and there they were: flayed
by the light, screaming like geese

all shrunken and hairless. But they are kneading
my gift. Perhaps it's the longer days,
or the night, deep beneath, has rays
of its own—yet they are baking and feeding

somehow. Bits of bread
have come out of the basement drains, clogging
the holes. Spiders emerge with soggy
crumbs in their arms, their heads

devouring them whole. Little crusts
are caught in the legs of centipedes, who scramble
out of corners, gorging on the damp hills
of grain mixed with dust.

The sewers have rats now, I've heard,
that, if you shaved their whiskers, would remind
you of the ruddy cheeks, and the smiles, the shining
eyes and gaze, the assured

hopes of a farmer's boy
standing by his mother's oven, waiting.
I admit: I used flour with bugs in it. It was late.
So they are eating their friends; but enjoying it!

BEAUTIFUL TIME

I wonder about the love
behind the brown-green toad
who lingers by the road,
dusty, the whole world above.

He is waiting for a sewer
or a placid dirty pond
where, having made his song,
the world will be one toad fewer.

It seems that beauty glows
only for a moment. Once seen
it washes away in the green
water of the long gutter's flow.

BIRTH TIME

When Herod announced his Bethlehem raid,
he surely didn't have someone like the babe
Willie in mind.
He was after the Messiah, a very different kind
of child—
which is partly what is so odd about the thing:
who wouldn't want God as their king
right then and there?

I would happily let someone control the air
I breathe so long as it's clean. Well, fair
enough: it's senseless.
That is, Herod kills the babies, hence
he's mad.
But there seem to be quite a lot of such
people around, touched
in the head, these days.

So what? Maybe he was not so crazed
after all? It's easy to get caught in the maze
of likelihoods: you could
do this or that maybe . . . I'm not too good
at figuring
this out: something beautiful exists
in the world, but it's a risky
business, isn't it.

At the birth of W. K., 2012

Chasing the Shadow

BONE TIME

I.

From unseen to unseen there is a bridge
made up of thin and brittle bones.
As you swing along, your eye lids
flutter in the wind, your gaze roams

into the sky all round you.
Mothers, fathers, children span
the dark and the sound you
hear, the cracking, the grand

dissolving . . . hold on! hold
tight! the birds scream, their wings
thrashing by your face. Too cold
above, too warm below, they sing;

steady as you go, they sing;
press forward, they sing.
Veering away, leaving you swaying,
they still sing.

II.

"May his bones be ground to dust,"
the Rambam sharply said.
The hated Nazarene was dead
a thousand years now; lust
and flesh for Moshe too
awaited Mashiach's touch.
Meanwhile, the wicked Jew
Yeshua chose to trudge
through filth, its flakes of skin,
its dusty bones thrown in a hole.
Only then he's free to win
Maimonides' astonished soul.

At night he nibbles at my fingers,
the sound of his teeth a kind of singing.
At dusk he waits by the fence,
seeing what crumbs the gods will send.

III.

At dawn he scurries back to the pails
of dark garbage, piled by the railings
of the basement stairs.
One day they will find him, his hair
fallen away, his skin taut,
his now tiny skeleton, wrought
in mystery, ready to break
in pieces and crumble away.
At last, bits of rat, resembling
dust, will join the great assembly,
carried upwards, angels flinging
them to the sky, bones ringing.

Chasing the Shadow

CAT TIME

I met a cat
on my window ledge.
And there he stood
on the flowered ledge
two hundred feet above.

"Cats don't fall,"
my wife politely said.
Yet I found one
upon the pavement, dead
and with its legs all splayed.

Its head lay softly
to the side, while ants
were gently stepping
on one eye, a dance
I watched, but no one heard.

Above him soared
a palace, whose windows winked
and smiled in the light.
I sighed. What could I think,
but that the wind was strong?

"Come close," I said;
"and I will take you in."
He turned the corner, floating,
tail swinging, the thin
red flowers swaying.

CHILD TIME

I.

No matter if the earth should puff and spin
itself into a frenzy, warming to the touch,
her oceans will run cold and colder still
below their upper currents and their rushing
streams. Far down, as darkness grips a long
descent, the sparkling eyes begin to fade,
glimmers weaken, all becomes a pressing hush.
The sunken tides stretch out the belly of the
world, sliced only by quick movements of the
ribbon fish and snipe eels, or by sleek red
vampire squid, who dart unseen above
huge isopods and giant, silky tube worms,
blossoming in their silent galaxy.
Here, in the deep waters of His heart,
from which all creatures find their hidden start,
He tugs them out with honed precision, one
by one, placing each creature in the sun,
showing it off before His courts. It glitters!
Look what He has brought into the light!
Fang-toothed anglers, frilled sharks, starry chambered
nautilus, reflecting from below
the quartz of mountain tops, and all the shining
grasses of the hills. See what has come
from the abyss, the storehouse of His grace:
such things as children, softly singing;
such things as my daughter's gentle face.

II.

When you get old enough,
we say goodbye and let you go.
Every parent does this.
Knowing it creeps up behind.
We come to expect it and wait for it glumly.

Chasing the Shadow

But we lose a part of us
that you then take away, whistling—
an arm, a leg, an eye.
What happens to it we have been trying
to guess, but can't figure out:
you put it in a jar of alcohol,
wrap it in a bloody shirt,
stuffed in the back of a deep drawer,
or, like the books on our basement
shelves, one distracted day
you cart them out in boxes,
wondering if you ever read some.
Maybe you did once,
but it's like a tune you can't quite place.
But we are more for our losses,
and you, for the packages you've lightly tossed
aside in the hall closet.
We are better for the hobbling and groping, and you
for forgetting and looking away.
Like the fields, that are so rich and deep
when you dig down and finally see:
the layers never speak, know,
or remember much from another time;
sorghum grows across
the old ruts above, the flies
dancing, the lizards nibbling
at the ants who are crawling in and out.
One night you lie down and look up:
there is so much above and underneath,
even pressed inside
from all the hidden corners, the jars,
the boxes, and old shirts,
now dried out, frayed and brittle.
Then your heart melts.

III.

Forever doesn't mean much when compared

to the life of a flower, just here, not anywhere.
Out beyond Pluto, everything can be seen—
the long darkness, a few points of light,
barely throbbing, vague cool green
haze, drifting away into the night.
Turning backwards to the little orb
that sits aimlessly hidden in its corner,
mottled blue, tufted, listing towards
its final fire, but now only warming
its hands while it whistles a small careless tune,
one realizes how few flowers there are in all
the universe—so few that each of them could soon
be counted by one man. Not even a small
god would be needed to make a full list.
Bromes and buttercups, harebells and tiny asters,
lilies and bedstraws—you could hold them in your fist.
On the edge of this great stretch of quiet that has mastered
everything, stems and petals have appeared, tinctured
and trembling before their impossibility. I have climbed
above nine thousand feet, and taken in my fingers
a small gentian, purple and blue. I'm
sure these have something to do with you.

Chasing the Shadow

CHURCH TIME

The holy catholic Church,
in case you didn't know,
has flesh that's on its way
where everybody's flesh will go.

She struggles to come forth,
stretching out her head
from deep inside the dark,
preceding, soft, white bed.

Her matted, moist first hairs
are toweled clean and dry.
She teeters, then she runs,
awkward and reaching as she cries

in the expectant light.
The cough and fevers beat
against her lungs and heart,
but still she runs on through the streets

her arms grasping out ahead,
her legs in lengthening strides,
the air still pure to drink,
the earth still firm. So flesh abides.

She bears her burdens now.
She wields her axe and scythe
on trees and fields. The noise
shudders the brush and birds arise,

calling in the air.
She lifts her head to smile
at their rippling songs.
And this is the joy that lasts for a while,

while even the heart inside
begins to roam and harden,
while even the smile lies,
and she sneaks in the backdoor, dripping and tardy.

So love and lust make war,
and love is what she asks
to be the stronger. Thus she prays
and faces into the wearying tasks.

Until the steps begin
to slow, the sun to linger
in a thin and acrid light,
spread across the air with a finger,

only the weakest layer
of red on a dusty day.
Now she may truly cough,
now she may sit at length. She may.

Others pass her by.
The water in the belly dries.
Skin shrinks, and blood must sigh.
It seems she sleeps without even trying,

as she sits in a chair,
as the air no longer flows,
as the mountains settle
to her size, as the flesh goes.

But not to where she came
does she return. The dark
at the beginning's not the same
as the burning that the end will mark.

Chasing the Shadow

CONFESSION TIME

I threw a shovel to the mice.
For weeks they had been at it, their eyes
flickering in the leaves and woodpile.
It was a tough winter.
Their teeth were splintered
and they were worn and fading,
their fur graying into tips of white.
They needed help; and who doesn't, right?

Things picked up after that.
It was hard to imagine, glad
as I was with only a crust
of snow on the ground
and mostly the sounds
of a clear sky.
Yet underneath: corridors of space,
room after room, tunnels and caves!

They were putting everything away
and no one knew, though you could say
it was the reason the air was clear.
Everyone wants angels,
as if things will change
only from above
instead of being sucked in and ranged away!
Yes: *inside* are the friends, the universe, and day.

DAVID'S TIME

When David became old
and his feet, gnarled and cold
under the covers, were white
and heavy, Abishag's light
form wrapped his flesh
so that he could rest.
She took his bones and kneaded them
while Adonijah seated
himself where his father once
gazed and judged the sum
of his people's hearts, where the Law
of God hovered, where he saw
his own sons and wives
parade before him, their lives
spilled from the one throne.

And this is when David groaned.
This is when the mud
in his veins loosened and the blood
ran down to his ankles with a red
blush, when the sheets of the bed
were opened. This is when
David ceased to rend
his clothes, or cover his face,
or lie on the earth and trace
the soil with a teared finger.
For he had been a singer
of songs, and their notes were streaming
away now. He was leaning
forward, as if to stand.
He began to walk. Then he ran,
the blankets dragging behind,
and groped as he sought to find
his children somewhere before him.

Chasing the Shadow

    But now, at last, it is warm.
    As from a shadow torn
    out of the place where he began,
    he reaches out his hand.

DEMONIC TIME

Wine makes glad the heart of man
and beer is the belly's friend.
I will drink while the mountains tumble and quake
and the stars course to their end.

Drink too while the young men are taken away
and the children are left on the floor,
while the maidens are petted and handled
and then they return for more.

I'll lift a glass while the pillars
of justice are shaken below,
and the righteous turn to each other
wondering where they can go.

While the walls of the vineyard crumble
and the boar has ravaged the vine,
while people gaze at the sunset
squinting at Jonah's sign.

While companions who sat at the table
betray the hands that broke bread,
while close to the bosom's friendship
there are teeth and spittle instead.

But I am only somewhat a man
and have only somewhat a cup.
I'll pour it across the nation's fields
and they shall lick it up.

Then they shall sing my simple song,
the new song that will free
the flesh and turn the tongue to join
the lips of stones and trees.

Chasing the Shadow

The lips of stones and trees part wide,
and their tongues begin to trill,
and we who are somewhat men—and gods!—
will drink till we've had our fill.

DOG TIME

He shall let it be a lair
for jackals. Where?

Here—on the lawn with its trees
dipping in the breeze

in front of the house, its teak
door creaking.

In the silent mall's parking
lot. It's dark;

just a few lamps
dot the ramp

to the second level. That's right:
now it's night.

Or, in the long grass
winding past

the side of the canal,
slightly sallow,

with bits of trash peeking
out from the sleek

wild blades. It's about
noon. Watch out!

Maybe just the vacant lot.
The one they've got

next to the great, big tower,
its glass glowering

Chasing the Shadow

on the gasping sycamores that cling
to the little ring

of stones that count as a square.
That's exactly where

the café, the parents, the bar,
and the child are.

No one is looking now.
This is how

the long stretches we thought
were ours—we bought

them, after all!—have spread
into a bed

for wandering dogs. High
and low they cry.

Hills, fields, and sand;
all of the land.

DRUNKEN TIME

There is a nightclub down the street
called The Baobab.
The name suggests an oddity:
the most beautiful trunk of twisting,
enveloping life in the world
is watered by beer and piss.

And the suggestion gets it backwards.
These tiny, swaying, bending
bones of ours, cracking
against the wooden bar
or on the concrete pavement,
whose slivers finally shed
into the powdering leaves,
draw up their whitened force
from the tree's deep roots;
our awkward turns reflect
only a little its massive
curvature and untroubled poise.

And year after year, it pees on *us*,
its yellowed leaves dropping,
dissolving in the air,
as we fall on the ground with our tongues
licking the sticky soil:
at last I am no longer thirsty!

EARTH TIME

When he was young, his hair grew fast,
tight at the crown in thickets, but vast
and flowing like fountains down the sides, flung
around his shoulders in a shawl that is hung

loosely, but warm, and dripping green
into the orbits of his brothers. He seemed to sing,
shaking his locks, and their rising steam
glinted and rippled through the darkness.

We will ask about the story of these stars
whom the prophets announced before the wars
came. There was Delilah, who crept
into the warmth of his arms, while he happily slept.

She whispered her anisette and lavender into the hush
of the evening, as she quietly cut his lush
strength away. Then she rushed
outside into the burning sun.
"Murderer!" he cries, as she runs.

Or did the earth himself become
a rebel, marshalling the hoards of his glum
followers against his father, who had fled
into the barren valley? And as the red

glow of the morning spreads, he is caught
in the great tree, his curls tautly
wound in its gathering arms, splayed
in the air, hurled to the blades.

Then it is our turn to mourn
our would-be murderer, like so many, torn
between duty and affection. In any case,
he is older now, with a worn face,

his hair thinned. At the city gate,
what's to weigh? Just shuffling. It's late.
We look up into the skies' arcade
of bald old men, grimly
spinning and twinkling dimly.

FAMILY TIME

Each morning when I walk by
the old men on the porch of the group home
say hi,
gripping their coffee in thought or
tilting the head, looking elsewhere at the absent
daughter
from long ago, or the forgotten
sibling, whose calls went unanswered, what?
it's been
thirty years? More.
They remember the block with the big trees and old
Ford
parked on the corner, rusting,
where they all grew up. But nothing in between.
It must be
what grace is like, seeping
into these great dark holes, piling
in heaps.

FRIENDSHIP TIME

What a glorious hummingbird I saw this morning.
Green sequins adorned
its small body, tight and shimmering
as it vibrated in the light.
Three feet from my raptured eye,
it sucked and captured the blue columbine's
liquor, weightlessly, invisibly,
unsated, the air undulating with its wings.
Then another flew in,
tinted blue, its long beak
glinting like an Aztec dart
waiting to be shot through the startled forests.
The sky exploded around them
as they fought, their small throats pounding
soundlessly in the sun.
They pulled back, then lunged and swerved
around the cool buds.
When they left, each on its own search,
far apart, unhurt, too hungry
to be exhausted, there was only the open
sky, lost over the blossoms,
a small, loose and wafting breeze.
In a few minutes, we will leave
together down the dirt road
into town, everything quiet again.
That's the direction of the creek
on its single trek into the valley,
while the sky, barrelling, open,
running everywhere, is flying above us,
and we trudge the same little path.
I am not complaining.

GROWING UP TIME

The history of my curtain:
I'm not certain of its childhood.
There would have been brown fingers,
Bleeding and reaching while singing,
then plucking and piling high.
They carried the cotton for miles,
Staring ahead, with sweat
running down and glistening
in the brown Bengali sun.
Who recalls their youth?
We forget the tall machines
now, and the hollering din
of the dim halls, the clanking,
the tired, falling heads
aching as they steadily
filled the long crates
with milled bolts and bales.

The tale picks up here.
When the cloth finally made port,
someone kind took it in,
looked it over, combed
its hair, brought it home,
dressed it in a bare coat,
edged with notes of lace.
I fetched it for my window.
Now the story begins:

For years, I think, a light,
just a small chink of light
would crawl into the square
of lace where it would hang.
Sometimes a breeze would chase it
through, the light wavering
in the folds. Or a heaving wind
would hold the cloth, wrapped

in coils, soft and clinging.
The curtain would swing about,
as if shouting wildly and happily
while the rain rapped the sills,
slapping the air outside.

My curtain stares out agelessly.
The children far away have faded,
their brown fingers stilled.
Their pounding heads have quieted.
It was a different time.
It has drifted into long ago.

Chasing the Shadow

HISTORICAL TIME

Yesterday is done, and who knows why?
Yet tomorrow is how yesterday will fly
and take her wing. Tomorrow too is done,
for by the bell of yesterday is long since rung.
What are these ears for but to hear the sounds,
the chords made by the two, entwined and bound,
criss-crossing, planted, hung, the joke of Greek,
where Jews fall down, the endless wailing of the weak?

INTERFAITH TIME

Mombasa is some ways away
but I was there just yesterday
while the rains still fell upon the hills
where, though late, some women were tilling.

The Christians and the Muslims walk
within the mist, their voices mocking
each other, through veiling tones with rustling
smiles, while their inner muscles

clench and wait until the time,
the day, the hour when each will find
the other sprawled across the pavement of the market
washed in red, or in the dark

port, fumes of diesel and of fruit
hanging in the rain. Who shoots
first? I watched, waiting for a ride,
a taxi, its driver asleep, idling.

There are no Jews here, though farther north
they range, just at the source
of Ethiopia, high on the cliffs.
From there, a great sea without mists!

But here! Here, not far from the tin
roofs and the angry stares, the thin
loaves, thinly spread among
the old, the restless hoards of the young—

here, they will merely beat their faith
into a dust that later tomorrow will grey
the waters, or mix with the daily rains
and make the songs all sound the same.

Chasing the Shadow

    Still, the ships will go forth and they will drift
    through the district of bandits while their load shifts
    with every rise and swell, and we shall wait
    for the prophet who comes when it is late.

JERUSALEM TIME

It is four o'clock.
Fifty men rush into the square, proclaiming.
It is hot.
Their words lie flat on the stone street,
like cakes baking.

It is five o'clock.
Fifty men rush through the alleys, singing.
It is dark.
The notes clatter against the walls,
like shadows cracking.

It is six o'clock.
Fifty men rush to a corner, shouting.
It is tense.
The lights of the police cars surround them,
like a fence flashing.

Oh, the hour! The hour!
Who is the god of this hour?
"My God," says the sparrow,
who flies up to the cornice of the ancient wall,
not falling,
like the wisp of a hair floating
high above the ground.

KNOWLEDGE TIME

I wanted to tell you something before you left
but fell asleep, so it never happened.
I have wracked my mind to recall
but it disappeared in a dream.
We were climbing a hill, in long grass
with small oaks dotting the edges
A white moth fluttered up into the wind,
and light clouds were dissolving,
opening to a deep blue beyond.
The faint outline of the moon drifted above,
like a backdoor opening to some dark ocean.
Everything I know is there.

MARRIAGE TIME

I.

You are not in my dreams.
When the drapes have closed,
knotted at the seams,
and the chill seeps and grows,
you do not haunt me.
The wind, the long trees,
the empty plains
that my dark doors open,
do not contain
your shadows or tokens.
When I am chased off the ledges,
run down the flat roads
lined by thick hedges
or by grass, unmowed
and rank, that is not where
you are. The dogs got there
first, come out from the woods
each one waiting, then slowly
approaching with red eyes and looks
of fury, while I roll
my head, gasping for a way
beyond, and the path
squeezes me like clay,
the sun a dry shaft
of dust over a grey river:
I stop there and shiver,
trembling as I lean
over the deep tide.

But you are not in my dreams.

Only when morning has sighed
a little and sneaks in,
only when the sheets rustle

and a leg stretches into the leaking
air, glistening as we shuffle
gently in the rake of light,
only when your hair brushes
against my back, untightening,
and one finger trails against the hush
of my skin and another meets
it there and our eyes seek
each other, gleaming.

You are not in my dreams.

II.

We hung the picture together.
When you slipped downstairs,
I stayed a moment, nudged
the frame to the left a bit,
then lay my palm against the wall,
cool and smooth like marble.
Pressing my cheek up now
to the surface, it was as if my face
had entered a hushed cave.
I could hear the insides of the house,
its veins and arteries, rushing:
bits of plaster dust falling and rising,
mice racing to their children,
forgotten voices, still faintly echoing.
The sound of a glass,
clattering in the sink
below where you had gone,
rose up, and spread around,
like sparkling blood
running and running.
The picture seemed to tingle.
The whole house
was alive at last, like us.

III.

We gather our regrets
like wet snow on the runners
of a sled, packed up
until it sticks and stops.
In the middle of the woods,
we stand and scrape it off
the pale sun fading out,
our faces going numb.
At almost 60 years
my own have piled up;
shivering in the cold,
my boots have iced and stiffened,
like my slowed and stony hands.
You've somehow gone ahead,
but paused, tramped back to me,
taken out your knife,
knocked away the ice.
Your movements are small and quiet
as the dark settling and whispering.
We start again. I live
because you've lived a little
longer; a year of patience
more, your hands kneaded
with one more winter's work.

IV.

. . . Love . . . ,
it doesn't rhyme well. And we have roving
eyes, it seems. Even the doves
will fly about over bluffs
and towers, the sky streaked with mauve
at evening, while we are remembering the rebuff
of the morning, biting our lips, with our gloves
wiping our eyes. "That's enough,"
we say. So I will breathe in, toughen

up, come to your back at the stove
and put my hand on your shoulder and cough.
When you turn around, I will say how awful
it has been all day. You will think of shoving
me away, but will pause just briefly . . .

V.

I was looking for something to do—
strolling along the river, singing,
trailing my finger in the water—I'm through
with all this sort of thing.

The leaves of the tree spreading
apart, with the sun's bits spilling
on the path—walking there, I read,
was enough beauty to fulfill

even a savage. Like me,
I suppose. But I am still ruthless,
prowling, aimless among the trees,
albeit fading in tooth

and claw. Nothing works.
So I have come back to you. See:
in this small clearing, where nothing lurks,
I'll stand still. No more trees.

VI.

We've been crossing many creeks.
They have all been clear, though streaked
with the colors of tiny sand pebbles
glinting where they have settled.

Small rocks sit in the middle,
resting, and the water trickles
over their surfaces. Our feet are steady.
Sometimes, a branch has caught, or a heavy

log, wobbling where the current swirls,
white or golden. It's like uncurling
my fingers and brushing them over your legs,
slowly, lightly, when we are quiet, just awake.

That is how we walk: I trace
the small veins and eddies, the places
where your skin so slightly rustles,
shimmering with a thousand tiny muscles.

Inside, covered by the years of layered
flesh, are the rivers, the rushing conveyers
of blood, washing away all they grip
in their flood, everything they have ripped

away. The old arteries hidden within.
Their strong currents are muddy. They have been
taking everything. Nothing waits.
The bottom is invisible, and the great

waters mask the departure of prairies,
of mountains, homes, shores, all buried
where every river ends: in the sea.
There the world fades perfectly.

So I cross the rivers quickly, on a bridge,
looking behind only from a ridge
high above. But I will stand beside
the creeks and wonder as they glide

by. Then I will step on that small
rock, wait with you as the hush falls,
as the sound wrinkles the leaves of the hills,
as every tiny thing stands out, still.

Chasing the Shadow

MINING TIME

Long ago and twelve full miles
from any sort of road,
they buried Phillips William Symons
at 10,000 feet in Winfield, Colorado.
There are two dozen others with him,
cousins in enterprise,
who lie among the rocks and woods.
He came to dig for gold, not wisdom,
leaving prison and two children
in Ohio whom he never told
or knew, long dead
before him with their mothers.

This is what a man does:
He leaves, he digs, he wields his ax
to raise a house, its rough logs sealed
with tar, its insides blackened
by a fire lit against the snows,
with one bed, one shelf, one cup
and a blue tinned plate,
useful for a few thin years.
This is what a man does.

Today, the snowmobilers race along
a small track through the woods.
The freezing air bites on their faces,
bits of ice and flakes of snow
streak against their cheeks.
Hidden in the tilting branches,
glorying in the white,
they remove their heavy helmets
so that the roar of their machines
becomes a world,
seamless with the wind.

Here is freedom:
this flight into the woods,
the whipping passage,
the wind and unprotected faces,
the machines that span the whitened spaces
left between the freezing trees,
the small roar
sputtering out over the graves.
Here is freedom.

Chasing the Shadow

PEACE TIME

Among other things, my father told us
to dress well when doing something important,
like praying or singing the old hymns,
or for meeting and addressing important people,
like God, perhaps a bishop,
maybe a colonel in the army:
men should take off hats and wear ties,
women unfaded cloth, arms covered.
When they look at you, as you stand still,
they should feel calm and well-being,
like smooth hills and fat cows.
This is how he would bring the Bible, appealing
to people in the tangled bushes near the river.

And what he said is all true, more or less:
when they strangled him in '72, he had no fear;
he was dressed in a tie, which they used.

But we have mainly had peace since 2004,
which was not long after, at least as the Bible explains things.

Pierre Nkunrinziza, Burundi's president, on his father's death

PRAYER TIME

The horse is standing in the shade,
eating from a faded bag of grain.
His cart is loosed from his sagging back,
propped on the soiled, black pavement.
Next to it, as it munches food,
his driver hunches over on a mat
in the middle of the street.
His head touches the heated ground.
The blaring chant announces,
with its electric echo and panting whine,
God, who is great, who is great,
who is great. And the waiting horse
is eating, eating, and eating.
The sun slides like treacle down the gutter,
slowly spreading itself out
over the rocks, the loud trash, the dust.
It oozes into the cracks and fills them
up with its spilling warmth and light.
Like a sheet of snakes, it twists
into the corners, hissing as it runs
up the walls, jumping the sunken curbs,
covering the tall, tottering apartments
and turning them into a glittering skin
of throbbing, writhing plaster. It grins,
yellow, massive, and master of all,
alive, alive, alive.

Alexandria, 2014

Chasing the Shadow

PROPHET TIME

We sat at the table.
The meat was passed around.
As I held the platter and the ladle
For the sauce, there was a clattering sound:

he had dropped his fork.
Now he was staring straight
ahead, even while the pork
glistened in my hands. "It is late,"

he intoned, as if raised
from the dead, and now blinking
in the light, his face astonished and dazed.
"There is fire everywhere! The mountains are sinking

into the seas!
Oh, the land! Oh,
the land! Even the sun flees!"
He fell silent, while my father took a slow

breath, then
shifted in his seat
and gave my uncle a glance. When
a moment had passed, he said, "I'll have some meat."

ROCK TIME

Water is in the rock.
She leaves her messages there.
Whenever the stone asks her to talk,
she unburdens all her cares

to him, as he sits down
and listens. There is a lot
to say, and there are many sounds
that the water inside the rock

pours forth now. She shudders and sobs
as she speaks of the sun and the stars
before she entered into the rock,
before the endless wars

in which he was trampled or thrown
down the hillsides or into the pock-
marked walls of the town, guns droning.
It was inside *this* rock

that she had gone and drawn
with her the sparks from the shock
sent out long ago by the earliest dawn.
And so she placed in this rock

shy blue droplets that told
of her hopes and of what was not
to be. But the passage she followed from the old
origins into the rock's

young heart had been difficult, its plot
was tangled amid the spinning
planets, her messages left in the rock
were garbled, and as if beginning

Chasing the Shadow

> on his own, he had groped his way
> down slopes or through the bogs
> and the fields, still trusting that maybe one day
> she would speak. And inside the rock
>
> she did, bit by bit. She talked
> to him softly, and spoke of her own
> long journey, giving him courage. The rock
> grew stronger and suppler. And bones
>
> formed quietly in him. The water
> nestled inside of the rock,
> while he carried there the shape of his daughters.
> If you cracked him open and unlocked
>
> the fasteners of dust, you would find
> the water inside the rock
> swirling about young animals, with their fine
> faces, tiny and dotted
>
> with eyes and ears, with their small
> fingers and feet. You would spot
> their hair and their teeth. They would be crawling
> about, there in the rock's
>
> own center. This you would see:
> herds and teeming flocks.
> It is hard to know how it came to be
> this way: water in the rock.

SEA TIME

The small crab found a pool
tinted pink and purple
with the thin grass from the cool tides
of the sea.

Twice a day, sometimes,
it sparkled in the sun.
When the waves roared overhead
at other times

he hid behind a tiny
rock, and said, "how beautiful
is my home!"

The bird who took him was
a cormorant.
She would glide
down from the cliffs above,
jabbing in

the surf or settling on
a current for a moment,
Then rise up high, with the years
lifting her wings
until the day

they finally pressed her into
the rock and left her there.

At the very top, a little
boy gazed out over
the huge and glimmering waters.
He breathed in deeply,

Chasing the Shadow

    As far as his young lungs allowed,
    and sighed. "I shall be a sailor!"
    he murmured in a yearning gasp.

    The sea below pushed on,
    fixed its eyes upon him,
    "Mine!" he said softly.

    Port Eynon, 2015

STROKE TIME

My friend went down to the subway
after a busy day
and when they took her out again
it seems that she had stayed

two hours there, and night
had fallen. She had sat
on a bench, while another train would pass,
the doors just opening at

her feet. Every four minutes
one direction, four
again the other way. Although
who knows if there were more

than thirty trains who passed
her by? The people pressed
around her bench—water rushing
around a stone at rest,

loosed by a force upstream.
Around and around, while
a TV monitor hung above
with pictures about trials,

another war, you recall,
in the Caucasus, of rage
and widows, another subway with bombs—
in two long hours, this age

and all its ills had passed,
though every train was new
and no two people were the same.
The reach of the tunnels grew

Chasing the Shadow

    like stars that have stayed too long,
    sucking their own light,
    churning away. Some day they will find
    two workers, wedged in tightly

    where the waters meet in a hole
    like Hezekiah's. My friend
    was seizing wildly on the bench
    and just around the bend:

    the thirty-first train.
    The stars were far away
    when they took her to the air outside,
    masked by a gauze of grey

    clouds. She took her head
    in her hands, and still the pounding
    carried on. "What am I hearing?
    What have I heard?" The sounds

    of a young girl, marrying.
    Only that. The grass
    of the Caucasus. Doors opening.
    Dark stars passing.

SUFFERING TIME

I will wait for you here. You will rush
through the thickets and run across the wide field, whose stones
hit your feet, jutting up from the grass and throwing
you sideways. Then you will climb the big hill, brush

giving way to scattered trees, which clear at the top.
I will try to remember what it is like: the grappling;
the smeared lines of green on your hands from the sapling
leaves and thin branches you pulled at; you stopped

to catch your breath, looking through the gap
in the hills at a deep blue, with a wave of wind
briefly wiping your face; you are tired and your shins
ache from the pounding; still, you have come, with no map.

It was just like this for me, perhaps. It's late.
I barely recall these things. Besides, I can wait.

Chasing the Shadow

SUICIDE TIME

"Treat me nice, or I will kill myself,"
the woman said; and that's how she was treated.
And all is well, for nothing else was needed.
This was the gift Mkwawa gave his people
as he placed the Arab rifle to his
chin and pulled the trigger. Do not think
the Germans cared! Ever glad to let
someone dispatch himself without their sweat.
But that's the sheerest beauty of the thing!
Think of the gift to families that it brings,
where death becomes the shield against revenge
and calm the fruit that comes on either end
in any case. "To hell with you, to hell
with me!" will cover all our sins and draw
a veil of concord on the warring hills.
Lay an endless railroad by corvée
or slap your spouse—there's peace the Hehe way.
The violence ceases when it's you you kill.

Among the Hehe of Tanzania

SUMMER TIME

There is a beach with children on it,
a wonderful, open reach
of blue, clutching at the land,
barely a cloud, red bonnets,
nakedness, light, and sand.

There will be a war, but now
no one knows this, nor cares.
How would they? They are running and swallowing the air.
The fishermen are home, and have dragged the prows
to the water's edge, as a fair

breeze rubs the colors against
each other. I can see
the shirtless old men and boys,
the small girls and someone who mends
his net, all joyous,

legs and sails all flapping and shouting.
The world is envious, trailing
behind with longing and with tender
looks. No one predicts or doubts.
No one even remembers.

Valencia, 1937

THEODICY TIME

We cannot make God the author of sin.
He is not, but rather sits within
his home by a large shimmering hearth.
Sin, a beggar, lingers apart
on the steps outside, the bitter night
driving him towards the quivering light
inside the flecked windows. He senses
the warmth behind the door, and bends
towards the lintel's narrow crack,
craving an opening. At the back
of the room, if the master would just unbolt
the latch, is the fire, and he could hold
his eyes upon the flames, sadly
imagining a comfort he will never have.
His hands are scratching the light, frozen,
reaching for his Lord's infinite repose.

TORTURE TIME

My cab driver was tortured by the police
in Iran. It took him years to find peace
of mind, and still it didn't show.
He drove slumped in his seat, his head low
to the window, mumbling all the way.
"I like everyone. But Muslims say
one thing and do another. Cheats,
liars, evil." Of course, the beatings.
"Why believe in God?" he added.
"Your name is all that lasts." He sadly
nodded to the road, which gleamed in the sun,
winding through the hills, streams running
into a lake we passed. I was off to catch
a plane. But there, rushing by hedges
and sheep, under small white clouds,
between two towns and their crowded
streets, rain-cleansed and hushed, were hills,
empty, green, and glittering. He turned still,
holding the wheel and listening. We were quiet
for a few minutes in the early light.

Chasing the Shadow

UTAH TIME

Like a plain:
this is marriage, someone said.
Maybe so,
but not with the brown hills of dead
joy or the fences
laid out as far as you can see,
the cattle resigned,
enduring in the fields their dumb virtue breeds.

Rather, a veil:
torn apart, with its trail of beasts
swarming through the breach
across the flooded earth from the East.

It would be a desert
if you stood up and surveyed it,
but if you stooped,
a teeming ocean with its thousand waves
trembling and crested
with red rocks and orange dust
flowing like water
running over the slopes and rusted
stones washed
with velvet ants and a spume of shimmering
carpet beetles,
like a fleet of tiny ships swimming
at the base of the cliffs—
They dot the bay of their ancient world,
that bursts with lupine
and swaying milkweed the wind has unfurled.

You see this as your lids
flutter in the sun, the leafhoppers flapping
among the buckthorn;
you press your face closer, tapping
the spurges with your lashes,

glimpsing the lizards that run about,
listening for their feet
that make the canyons quiver with small shouts.
Lie on your back,
flat in the saltbush, and gaze at the hawks
who eye your friends
close by in the weeds, irises taut.

This is the plain:
burberries, vetches, bee-flies and the rain
when it comes, driving
the assassin bugs into the holes again
with kitfox and quillpig.
You have lain down in it,
swum in it, been washed in it;
the big sky runs away, lost
before this tide
that sweeps across an old creation.

You were sent here,
far away from the small station
where they left you.
Now you are one with the speckles of sand
that make up the stars.
You have entered a wild, glittering land.
Marriage is a plain;
once made, forsaken, now reclaimed.

Chasing the Shadow

VICTORY TIME

The devil is a big monster who eats people.
I mean really big: like a mountain,
with a mouth larger than a canyon,
with teeth as sharp as the rocks
that line the summits and river beds.
He stands overlooking the plains
and gorges himself, small legs and feet
crumbling out of his lips in his haste,
tumbling over his bibless belly
onto his dripping toes.
Such an appetite, and so many
tiny creatures falling in bits!

Across a big river
all the saints have gathered and yell
at him, shaking their fists,
making rude gestures.
"Nyah, nyah, nyah!" they cry.
They mock in swelling unison.
The ground is shaking,
a rift is splitting through the rocks.
They are decreeing a new law:
Nyah, nyah, nyah!

The birds are swirling about
in between, circling, swooping,
back and forth over the river,
waiting to see where to descend,
gulls over a trawling vessel,
not yet come to port.
It is as if no one has told them,
and they are lost and drifting,
uncertain, uneasy.

WAR TIME

They are Germans in little boats
that sail under the sea.
That is what my cousin says
and what the big planes see

flying over, all last week
with Americans inside
who drop fire on them from above.
Why planes? Have they not tried

their big ships that I used to see
when I was a little boy,
long and made of metal? We paddled
out, the harbor's noise

rattling the water and the bananas
we had carried through the streets.
We burned our fingers on the metal sides
that had soaked up the day's heat.

I like the salt ships that I load,
their sails like birds in flight
over the long blue trail to the city,
like birds who spread their white

wings as they leave the hills of salt
below on which I stand,
my feet dried out and cracked—they fly
out to the sea, the land

left to the drying heat, the sea
swallowing up the brief
shouts of the Germans as they sink
into the rippling reefs.

Gonaives, Haiti, 1944

WEARY TIME

Somewhere I ceased to love.
In the garden, the spade became
only a spade.
In the ground where I had shoved it,
there was only dirt, flattened by the sun,
some dried blades
of grass, as if dropped from above
long ago, now rustling with the hum
a hot wind through the old house makes.

Somewhere I ceased to recall
the people who lived there, or when
they had packed their things
in a car or cart to haul
away. Did they have cars then?
Or did they slink
off on foot, a shawl
wrapped around the shoulders of their children,
as they climbed into the hills, tired and no longer thinking?

Somewhere I ceased to look
about me, but only stared.
I sat. It had been
the stoop, the boards crooked,
the heat pulling apart the bare
grain, a thin
ant pausing. I took
the path down to the road, where
someone passed, distracted, well-clothed, trim.

WIDOW'S TIME

There are three things to avoid:
First, eating meat that is cut with a knife—
flesh is always best enjoyed
using your teeth to tear apart its life;
Next, drinking water given you by someone else—
no, go to the spring and lap it up with your tongue;
Last, somebody's blood—the health
issues here are obvious, and anyway you're too young.

Death always comes from another person.
Didn't Cain kill Abel?
If we were only ourselves, first and
last of all, sitting alone at the table,
true just there: this is utter perfection.
I'm hardly suggesting that it's *right*.
To get this kind of effect, one
would have to be God or the like.

We were made to be with others,
and this is why we die.
The little love we have smothers,
or at least softens, the cries.

Chasing the Shadow

LENTEN TIME

1.

God, you have set me to wondering.
Each day, five questions come:
on waking, and seeing the world,
why am I so unsure?
on eating, is reality turned inside out?
on people, do they move their mouths
as if they had minds that are not mine?
if all is given, what is there to find?
how can I sleep, rustling and sighing,
and you not answer?

2.

God, you have a long history.
I have looked at your sheet
with its lists, traced in a neat
hand: a column of mysteries
side by side simple acts,
harsh judgments next to grace,
light, with deep smudges. In this case
I must sort fiction from fact.

3.

God, you have an eye
though you do not see.
You have a hand
though you do not touch
an ear and mouth
though you do not hear or speak.
You are a statue
towering, an effigy
denoting
that by which everything

is just like other things
all scurrying at your feet.

4.

God, you have smoothed the tree
that lies across the creek,
all its branches worn
down, its bark torn
off long ago, or crumbled
into the water, running
away downstream. A squirrel
scrambles over it, a whirl
of rain washes it. I am sobbing.
It is too slippery. I must stop.

5.

God, you have invented letters.
Each is something my mouth curls
around, delicious like a candied pearl.
As I speak, it tastes better and better.

Hel-lo!, I say, savoring
each syllable for you or another, whom
I will take to myself soon
enough, sweating and laboring.

6.

God, you have made the sea,
and all that is therein,
Is this where fish and oysters flee
the dried out mass of sin?
Deep underneath the light,
in caves without a breeze,
is this where those who cannot fight,
have finally found their peace?

Chasing the Shadow

7.

God, you have sent your Son into the world.
My own mouth has eaten up the words of the surly
crowd, milling about. "It's a wasted gift
from an old man, out of touch." "Stiff-
necked youth!" the Son, supple and broken, whispers
to me—"wait, simply wait; you are missing
before; and after, and today is not enough."
It's never enough, I said. Never was,
never will be. Never. "No," he said, "it isn't."
"Eternal inadequacy," he added. "That's my business."

8.

God, you have been gentle to me.
Is it possible to hurl lances and stones,
at you, yet all the while be flown
in some winged carriage of blooming
moss, at your command, just yours?
Even while every missile of my wrath
turns back at me, and rising up, you smack
it aside? You are gentle in your wars.

9.

God, you have dealt generously where you could:
sun and rain on the evil as much as on the good,
and so on. Could it be the trillion stars you name
are just for us, or we for them? That we are the same
for one another, nothing but pure gift and grace,
as you wend your way through the spaces?
Yet I lie down amid the leaves;
blown by the wind's cold winter.
together we dry out, grow thinner.
What is left to give or receive?

10.

God, you have stayed out late.
I know you told me, never wait.
I saw someone who knew you;
she said you hadn't called.
This is what your family's used to,
but most people are appalled.
In the morning you'll be sitting there,
at the table with a dish
full of bacon that you'll share
with me. The rest is for the fridge.

11.

God, you have crept down in Jesus
to have a look around,
to see and be seen.
Is it really easier this way?
Can I take his face in my hands,
tracing the lines of his cheek and jaw?
Skin for skin, Satan says.
Better just to listen.

12.

God, you have surprised me.
At every step, the ground opens,
the edges crumble and I hear
the rocks bouncing and rumbling
as they fall beyond sight and sound
below my feet.
To walk in this world is
to be confounded,
astonished, careful.

13.

God, you have reminded me
over and over again,
how, in the midst of this timelessly
offered world, it shouts "Amen"
to you, not once but always.
I am but rubbing at its sides,
running its turns and hallways,
listening to its cries.

14.

God, you have stood fiercely
in the face of your enemies.
You wear a mask, only your ears
sticking out, and wave your weaponry
so that it casts shadows
on their faces, and they freeze.
Gasping in terror, they throw
themselves down on their knees
begging for mercy. You keep
waving—clubs, spears,
arrows. Your cries are deep
and mix with their tears.
They listen, gulping and fumbling.
They cannot quite decide
if it is sheer power that is rumbling,
or just their own insides.

15.

God, you have been performing all week
at the place on the other side of town.
You attract a small crowd
of aficionados or, is it,
cognoscenti, or just plain
neighborhood layabouts,

who need a glass and a dark space
where they can sit, quietly
listening to you wander
about the keyboard,
leaning back
with your eyes closed.

16.

God, you have had a long journey
and are probably tired.
If you were not, why
go at all? There is learning,
stretching, aching, watching
that is part of any trip.
Here is water, to wet dry lips;
sitting down at a crossing,
delighted, mindless, spent.
That is why our home
is worth the effort. Unknown,
hard traveling will make us friends.

17.

God, you have let me keep speaking.
"When he's drinking,
why doesn't he hum?
When he's running,
why doesn't he whistle?
He says he is listening,
but all that leaks from his mouth
are growls, whines, claims."
What are you waiting for? The blame
to rise into a great
mass, sinking me with its weight?

Chasing the Shadow

18.

God, you have placed little Ceres betwixt
the planets of our dreams.
There, you are having mixed
drinks in a small and dreary
bar, but with good music.
No one knows where you are,
running the universe with a cigar
in your mouth, a little booze in
your hand, the orbits all fixed.

19.

God, you have scattered the plague
here and there. In Venice, it weighed
down the artists, all the musicians
died, even the rickety inquisition
stalled. Then Vivaldi came
throwing about his red mane
of hair before the girls,
his long fingers running and whirling
along the neck of a fiddle.
It was wondrous! He scribbled
away, ended in a pauper's grave
the girls still rustling their dresses
and sleeves as they played.

20.

God, you have pierced through the thick veil in your Son.
It was flesh he surpassed, riding it through the curtain
into the inner halls that, I am certain,
none of us have ever seen. He won

    enormous prizes for this, his blood spreading
across the heavenly altars, the marble glistening
in an angelic mode. They were all listening
of course—the angels that is—while stepping

lightly, joyfully. I really don't know what happened
there. Here, everything is still flesh.
The pools dry up eventually. Once fresh,
we only see things press on, then, tired, snap

in their dried brittleness. Winds rush over, things
drift away, the bits of cloth swinging.

21.

God, you have a habit of sneaking up on people.
"Boo!" you cry, waving your arms
from behind.
We smile, uneasily,
indulgent, uncertain,
knowing this must stop sometime.
But who will tell?

22.

God, you have sent your Holy Spirit
to keep me silent
to break my bones
to strengthen the tyrant
to veil the known
to hush my songs
to weaken my sinews
to wrench my calm
to squeeze out my tears
to harden my soul
to freeze my heart
O spirit of Christ
you are nothing but holiness,
holiness, holiness.

Chasing the Shadow

23.

God, you have stretched a skin
over the great drum of the sky,
striking it, so that the rumble
roars out; scraping it,
so that it screams across
the clouds, everything turning
bright yellow and pink.
We listen, enthralled,
standing in the wings,
gazing, astounded,
"There is nothing like it,"
we say to each other
as we leave.

24.

God, you have understood the smallest thought.
The ant wonders, yet you have made a lofty
tower from its tiny ken, that climbs
up to the moon and spreads its aureole finely
round the planets. On its filaments and threads,
all the gazing minds of spirits tread
ever so lightly, the worlds in their sights.
There goes the ant, fleeing from the white
heat of the sun, deep into the sand,
as if too weak to bear a thought so grand.

25.

God, you have been turning the earth.
Steam is rising from the mounds.
You have found small worms inside,
chewing the rocks, laying their remains
in little piles. Everything is straining,
pushing out, wriggling, reaching.
But before even the rush of their cries,

before their squeaks, and sighs leak out,
you turn it again. More earth,
more moisture, more tiny rustlings.

26.

God, you have remembered Zion.
You have wrapped your care within her stones,
where it waits, notes for another age.
Now they are built into the walls
of desperate families; now they line
the crowded streets, under the wheels
of trucks; now they are thrown hard
at police. Covered in white dust,
one day they will crack apart.
Out will spill secrets, promises,
the charts for everything important.
Can you read? someone will ask
a passerby. Let me see,
they will say, peering in,
then shaking their head and moving on.

27.

God, you have refused me wings.
Yet I defy you in my dreams,
casting off above ravines,
even the hardy would not lean
over. I pass above the coasts
that drop off into beaches. Most
seem small, until I glide down,
nipping the waves, catching their sound
before swooping up into the sun.
I let enemies drive me to rims that run
three thousand feet up, then I leap
and float beyond their grasp, sweeping
across the foolishness below and behind.
What will you do to me? Make blind
my sleep? Watch what I will find.

Chasing the Shadow

28.1

God, you have remade me
in the image of my wife,
and she in mine. If I could see
what this means for my life
everything would shrink
to the size of my hopes.
Instead, you are always thinking
of something else, and I am groping
to keep up. She's always
elsewhere, coming out
of the shadows, slipping away
before I am ready. I shout
at her to stand still,
but she is too fast.
If this is an image, it is one that will
always dissolve, never last.

28.2

God, you have made nothing as fine—
ever!—as this daughter and son of mine.
The whole world says this about its own.
They're right, of course. Each one has grown
like a single star, in a void. No one can line
them up. But my children are a sign
to the nations. Everyone should look and stare,
as if something marvelous, unheard of has dared
to appear. At last! people mumble, unaware
that stars are falling around them, like flares
dropping from a wild party in the sky.
A heaven of children, and one great lullaby.

29.

God, you have been thinking.
That is how the world goes:

your racing thought slows
to a brief inkling

of something blue and light,
swirling in cloths of clouds,
now spinning gently. You vowed,
with an arc striped in bright

colors, to stretch your reverie,
to hold it in time, throbbing
with hushed breath, bobbing
in an empty sea, where every

other shade is fixed,
and stares blankly. Think
on me! Consider our shrinking
orbit, and how sick

we have become. Do not
look away, distracted;
Concentrate! Act
as if there is a God!

30.

God, you have a closet
filled with clothes you never wear.
I know you worry about gossip,
or the way that people stare

at the unusually dressed.
I heard you once showed someone
who came over all the pressed
coats hanging, the fun

ties, with their faces
painted on, the silk shirts
that need a windy, open space
to flow. And yet you work

too much; always working
day after day. You never have time
to walk down the street, with your quirky
costumes. It's a crime.

31.

God, you have chosen Jacob as your own.
This explains everything:
Why rocks have edges;
why Jupiter is cold;
why the dog barks
 at 2 AM,
why a child disappeared
in dark Shamoken,
Pennsylvania and in
Wuwei, China
at exactly the same moment.
Why I am alive and someone
else died yesterday.
Why yesterday will
never be today.

32.

God, you have gone climbing.
pulling yourself up what you have made,
ropes and the rest.
You stare at the thin vines
straggling along the cliff, and small blades
of thin grass that press
out from dark cracks.
You hang there, running your hand against the rock
face, rough and striped
by washes of iron that track
to the valley floor. We walk
around the base, wiping

our feet in the mud, looking
up as you dangle high above us.
We are in the shade;
you are putting
your face into the sun. Come down! Enough!
we are impatiently saying.

33.

God, you have made one girl
out of the earth, moulding
dust and spittle, rubbing, twirling
in your fingers the folds

of her face, arms, back, long
legs. Then another
moulder came, singing songs,
caressing hair, reckoning

the hours and days of growth and duty.
Yet other moulders reached
in, smoothing, breaking, rooting
about the dark: teachers,

friends, devils and ghosts. Now
it's your turn, you said
to her: Mould yourself! But how?
she wondered alone. Can I thread

the calculus of hands that marks
my being? Figure the grand
design in this? It's far too hard.
One hand, please! Just your one hand!

34.

God, you have been watching the land.
Just here! Always, "just here."

Chasing the Shadow

    In and out the peoples ran,
    triumphant, dazed, or fearful,
    Parthians and Medes, the Elamites,
    and who knows what. The Jews rightly
    wonder about all this. "It's yours,"
    you said to them, but carefully lured
    in ruffians from the sweating East and South,
    hungering, stuffing children in their mouths,

    swallowing them whole or in torn bits.
    So what is anyone to think? You love
    the land, not the peoples. Once rid
    of them, you can finally rub
    the rough places smooth, and wipe
    the dust from the rocks, sweep up the white
    shards from the streets, plant trees,
    let the creeks swell, and the blue seas
    calmly lap the shores. Goats,
    conies, ravens, ants: hope.

35.

    God, you have gone up with a shout
    waving your hat, bucking away
    at the great heavenly rodeo.
    There you go, careening off
    one fence to another,
    up and up, like some
    untethered star,
    bouncing through the planets.
    So the worlds were formed.
    No one saw you, late at night
    nursing your bruises,
    soaking the dark spots,
    crying in the mirror.

36.

God, you have let the icebergs float on by.
We are all standing on the shore, watching.
They are gliding along, on some great
submerged current, while we are still.
The important things are passing,
yet here, everything has stopped.
We turn to each other: "are we moving?"
"No," we agree, and shake our heads.
Only the ice moves, and it is very cold.

37.

God, you have let me go on long enough.
This was to shake my hair, like a dog.
All the dirt, the fleas, the gritty stuff,
the wet film and matted sogginess,
hurled off. My limbs are loose,
readied for the long race.
Or perhaps it is another of your ruses,
and I am only lying prostrate,
lifeless, able to be pushed and pulled.
That is more than sufficient for this fool.

38.

God, you have come down from afar.
This is the one thing that could hurt you,
the Lord. You cannot simply assert it,
determine it, demand it. To be marred
in flesh and face needed to be won,
which was your great defeat.
Not even some divine deed
could suffice. It was all done
to you, by friends and lovers,
by children and the very innocent
you have protected. You spent
all you had. Everything hovered
in the balance, even your own fate.

It might have been emptiness, the end,
simple vanishing, Being sent
off. This time, in order to create,
you gave yourself away
to nothingness. Say
what you will, you nations:
this death is gracious.

39.

God, you have stayed with me.
After clawing through the opening
that you dug, you sat there,
gasping for breath, leaning
against the wall, with your eyes
closed, and your head back.
I stared at you, neither certain
nor happy. What did I know?
Had I asked for this?
When finally you sat up,
looked straight at me, and sighed,
I understood. For the first time
in six nights, I lay down
and rested.

40.

God, you have taken me with you.
When you pick up hitchhikers, first
you come to a stop before
opening the door, then ease
into the traffic slowly
staring straight ahead.
"I'm going about one hundred
miles on," you say,
"and you can get off where
you want." The motor hums.
Then you're quiet, gripping

the wheel, and we just go.
I can look out the window.
But because it's dark, I can hardly
see anything: fences
streaming by, dry
grass, and long open
spaces that gobble up
the night. "I'm grateful," I say
softly. And you nod.
"Getting off soon?"
you ask me. "No", I say.
No, not now."

Chasing the Shadow

EASTER TIME

1.

Even so in Christ shall all the waters pour forth,
overwhelming every dry valley.
We have waited for the rain for so long.

Lights, sun and moon, seasons, days and years, by the fourth
round of things, we were tired, awaiting the finale.
"Get to the blessed end, already." It's wrong

to make us hang on for a lifetime. It's as if you forced
us onto the king's ships, criminal galleys
with rows of oars, too wasted for the songs

the sailors sing above, chained together on a rough floor,
as the seas evaporate. "Pull!" the angels' rallying
cry goes in the heat. We're not strong

enough for this. We've been praying for a vast flood.
Something that will turn the earth into swarming mud.
Something that will lift everything up.

2.

Even so in Christ shall all lines meet.
Not so; though scholars make their sweeping
statements to this effect, it's tiresome.
Most of us suspect they are liars.
If we are not simply waiting,
blinking, gulping, still hating
all the while, we are pretending,
but with big words, bending
concepts from geometry and space.
All the special things have been wasted
in these games. Everything is made too small.
Not a point, but a crowd; not one but All.

3.

Even so in Christ shall all the hogs dance.
They shall put away rooting,
looking up instead, and singing.
They shall wear pants and frocks.
The fish shall clap their hands.
The rocks shall twirl and curtsey.
One moment of unleashing.

Then all things shall assume their proper stance.
The owls will be sage only as they hoot.
The scorpion will glisten only as he stings.
The dirty sheep will brighten only in a flock.
Water will roll only the tiny sands.
Israel and Edom will meet only in mercy.
One moment of perfect peace.

4.

Even so in Christ shall all the heaviness of the world
be rolled into one large stone.
Sisyphus and the heathen will find their home
clean and swept. Great Samson, moaning
in the rubble, will open his eyes. Goliath, prone
in the dust, will stand up. The fool, alone
with his wrath, after years of honing
his bitterness, will breathe out slowly. Builders, groaning
under the weight of their loads, will choose the lone
slab left in the quarry and carry it back, grown
strong and skilled like Bezalel. Again enthroned,
Abimelech will sit with his woman, grinning. From the foam
of the sea, violent Babylon will arise, intoning
its apologies lyrically. The scandalous too, thrown
into the ocean, will bubble up. And all the bones
the angels puzzle at, like seed sown
in the depths, will blossom, each joint known
by name, everything lifted up and blown
into the air, wafting to the ends of the world.

Chasing the Shadow

5.

Even so in Christ shall all the reds converge
into one field in the heavens, a great surge
of stain. They shall be swept in across all spaces
from the distance of every year, from every place,
rushing in after each moment, nothing missed.

They will be bled into a single disk
running from dark horizon to horizon, an edge
whose blade cuts the worlds from foot to head,
throbbing as it holds in its blushed charge.

It is ready to explode, its force enlarged
by the hand that holds it down, limitless,
inestimable.

Far away, the angels witness
all of it, their pores a-tingle, grieving:
We must go there one day! they weep.

"We too must be red!"

6.

Even so in Christ, shall all the flesh,
of beasts and men, filled with blood,
hidden and at rest,
free from cuts,

    sheltered from spills. It will secretly flow
    in every body, unstoppable, a private
    river, fast or slow,
    ever quiet

    like the Lord's hum. It pulses in our
    temples, as if the spirit were sweeping
    through, a strong swimmer
    while we sleep.

7.

Even so in Christ, shall all the wicked be gathered
into one place, seated on the ground
inside the huge wide stadium, surrounded
by empty seats; their knees drawn up,
their small sacks beside them, packed up
in a hurry with everything they thought mattered.

The guards stroll among the sullen crowd.
They have their swords drawn and are waving
them in the air, lightly, as if they are saving
their strength for what comes next: tribunals
counting the missing, relatives and corpseless funerals,
an international court, righteous and proud.

"Now you must kill us," the wicked say, grim,
trembling, resentful. Their pasty faces show
expectancy. "But you are free to go,"
the angels say, their swords bright like the air.
The bunched hordes stay put, staring
out, their knees pulled to their chins.

As the night comes, the wicked lie on their backs,
watching the stars inch into the darkness.
"No, but you must slay us," they whisper starkly,
"then be held to account. Just like us."
"But you are free," say the angels. "Trust us.
Here is some food, a stick for the road, hats."

8.

Even so in Christ shall all find their way home.
It will not be as they recall:
the ceilings taller, and the long halls
filled with light. The smooth stone

Chasing the Shadow

> walls will rise up, grabbing the hand
> to their surface. They will not recognize
> the pictures hanging there. The size
> of the chairs has changed. Plants stand
>
> in strange corners. The plates
> on the table have new patterns, ones
> with wild shades and lines that run
> onto the floor it seems. A great
>
> dizziness presses down and claims
> everything. So odd! Only the faint smell,
> creeping through the nose and chest, welling
> up through their fingers, is the same.

Bibliography

Achenbach, Shane. "A Teen Confronts her iPhone addiction." *Washington Post*, October 22, 2012. https://www.washingtonpost.com/national/health-science/a-teen-confronts-her-iphone-addiction/2012/10/22/3e2644c8-1306-11e2-ba83-a7a396e6b2a7_story.html?utm_term=.3838d3443a1a.

Anselm. *Proslogion: With the Replies of Gaunilo and Anselm*. Translated by Thomas Williams. Indianapolis, IN: Hackett, 2001.

Aquinas, Thomas. *Summa Theologiae*. Cambridge: Cambridge University Press, 2006.

Augustine. *City of God against the Pagans*. Edited and translated by R. W. Dyson. Cambridge: Cambridge University Press, 1998.

———. *Confessions*. Translated by R. S. Pine-Coffin. Harmondsworth, UK: Penguin, 1964.

———. *Expositions of the Psalms 99–120*. Translated by Maria Boulding. Hyde Park, NY: New City, 2003.

The Babylonian Talmud. Translated by I. Epstein. London: Soncino, 1935–52.

Banton, John. *Gleanings in Carmel: Being Thoughts and Observations on Select Passages of Scripture*. Stamford: Bagley, 1847.

Bate, Jonathan. *John Clare: A Biography*. New York: Farrar, Straus, and Giroux, 2003.

Bonaventure. *Itinerarium mentis ad Deum*. In *The Soul's Journey Into God; The Tree of Life; The Life of St. Francis*, translated by Ewert Cousins. New York: Paulist, 1978.

Bono, James J. *The Word of God and the Languages of Man: Interpreting Nature in Early Modern Science and Medicine. 1. Ficino to Descartes*. Madison, WI: University of Wisconsin Press, 1995.

Boyarin, Daniel. "The Gospel of the Memra: Jewish Binitarianism and the Prologue to John." *Harvard Theological Review* 94.3 (2001) 243–84.

Butler, Joseph. *The Analogy of Religion Natural and Revealed to the Constitution and Course of Nature*. In *The Works*, vol. 1. Oxford: Oxford University Press, 1849.

Child, G. Chaplin. *The Great Architect. Benedicite: Illustrations of the Power, Wisdom, and Goodness of God, as Manifested in His Works*. London: Putnam, 1867.

Clarke, Samuel. *A Discourse Concerning the Being and Attributes of God: The Obligations of Natural Religion, and the Truth and Certainty of the Christian Revelation*. 5th ed. London: W. Botham for James Knapton, 1719.

Collin, Francis. BioLogos Foundation. http://biologos.org/about-us/.

Coudert, Allison, ed. *The Language of Adam*. Wiesbaden: Harrassowitz, 1999.

Crome, Andrew. *The Restoration of the Jews: Early Modern Hermeneutics, Eschatology, and National Identity in the Words of Thomas Brightman*. Cham: Springer, 2014.

Bibliography

Daston, Lorraine and Michael Stolleis, eds. *Natural Law and Law of Nature in Early Modern Europe: Jurisprudence, Theology, Moral and Natural Philosophy.* Farnham, Surrey: Ashgate, 2008.

Davies, Paul. *God and the New Physics.* New York: Simon and Schuster, 1983.

Deckman, Melissa, and Joseph Prud'homme. *Curriculum and the Culture Wars: Debating the Place of the Bible in Public Schools.* New York: Peter Lang, 2014.

Eddy, Matthew D. "Nineteenth-Century Natural Theology." In *The Oxford Handbook of Natural Theology*, edited by John Hedly Brooke, Russell Manning, and Freser Watts. Oxford: Oxford University Press, 2013.

Einstein, Albert. *Ideas and Opinions.* Translated by Sonja Bargmann. New York: Three Rivers, 1982.

Hawkes, David, Richard G. Newhauser, and Nathaniel Bump, eds. *The Book of Nature and Humanity in the Middle Ages and the Renaissance.* Turnhout: Brepols, 2013.

Helmont, F. M. van. *The Alphabet of Nature.* Translated by Allison Coudert and Taylor Corse. Leiden: Brill, 2007.

Hunter, James Davison. *Culture Wars: The Struggle to Define America.* New York: Basic Books, 1991.

Jacobs, Joseph. "Are There Totem-Clans in the Old Testament?" *The Archaeological Review* 3/3 (1998) 145–58.

James, William. *Essays in Radical Empiricism.* New York: Longmans, 1912.

Jerome. *The Homilies of Saint Jerome, Volume 1 (1–59 on the Psalms).* Translated by Marie Liguori Ewald. Fathers of the Church 48. Washington, DC: Catholic University Press, 1964.

Kanigel, Robert. *The Man Who Knew Infinity: A Life of the Genius Ramanujan.* New York: Scribner's, 1991.

Kugel, James L. *Traditions of the Bible: A Guide to the Bible as It Was at the Start of the Common Era.* Cambridge, MA: Harvard University Press, 1998.

Kusukawa, Sachiko. "Illustrating Nature." In *Books and the Sciences in History*, edited by Marina Frasca-Spada and Nick Jardine, 90–113. Cambridge: Cambridge University Press, 2000.

Legaspi, Michael C. *The Death of Scripture and the Rise of Biblical Studies.* New York: Oxford University Press, 2010.

Levy, Ian Christopher. *Holy Scripture and the Quest for Authority at the End of the Middle Ages.* Notre Dame, IN: Notre Dame University Press, 2012.

———. "John Wyclif's Neoplatonic View of Scripture in its Christological Context." *Medieval Philosophy and Theology* 11/2 (2003) 227–40.

Lewis, Donald M. *The Origins of Christian Zionism: Lord Shaftsbury and Evangelical Support for a Jewish Homeland.* Cambridge: Cambridge University Press, 2010.

Macmillan, Hugh. *Bible Teachings in Nature.* New York: Appleton, 1967.

Marion, Jean-Luc. *Being Given: Toward a Phenomenology of Givenness.* Translated by Jeffrey L. Kosky. Stanford, CA: Stanford University Press, 2002.

Marrin, Albert. *The Last Crusade: The Church of England in the First World War.* Durham, NC: Duke University Press, 1974.

McInerny, Ralph. *Aquinas and Analogy.* Washington, DC: Catholic University Press, 1996.

McLuhan, Marshall. *The Gutenberg Galaxy: The Making of Typographic Man.* Toronto: University of Toronto Press, 1965.

Meer, Jitse M. van der, and Scott Mandelbrote, eds. *Nature and Scripture in the Abrahamic Religions: Up to 1700.* 2 vols. Leiden: Brill, 2008.

Mondin, Battista. *The Principle of Analogy in Protestant and Catholic Theology*. 2nd ed. The Hague: Martinus Nijhoff, 1968.
Neiman, Susan. *Evil in Modern Thought: An Alternative History of Philosophy*. Princeton, NJ: Princeton University press, 2002.
Ong, Walter. *Orality and Literacy: The Technologizing of the Word*. New York: Methuen, 1982.
Origen. *Contra Celsum*. Translated by Henry Chadwick. Cambridge: Cambridge University Press, 1953.
Pascal, Blaise. *Pensées*. Translated by A. J. Krailsheimer. Harmondsworth: Penguin, 1966.
Pedersen, Olaf. *The Book of Nature*. Notre Dame, IN: University of Notre Dame Press, 1992.
Primavesi, Anne. *Sacred Gaia: Holistic Theology and Earth System Science*. New York: Routledge, 2000.
Radner, Ephraim. *The World in the Shadow of God: An Introduction to Christian Natural Theology*. Eugene, OR: Cascade, 2010.
———. *Time and the Word: Figural Reading of the Christian Scriptures*. Grand Rapids: Eerdmans, 2016.
Raven, Charles. *The Creator Spirit: A Survey of Christian Doctrine in the Light of Biology, Psychology and Mysticism*. London: Martin Hopkinson, 1927.
Ray, John. *The Wisdom of God Manifested in the Worlds of the Creation*. London: Smith, 1691.
Schaff, Philip. *The Creeds of Christendom*. New York: Harper, 1931. Reprint, Grand Rapids: Baker, 1983.
Smith, William Robertson. *Lectures on the Religion of the Semites: First Series: The Fundamental Institutions*. Edinburgh: Adam & Charles Black, 1889.
Spencer, Archie J. *The Analogy of Faith: The Quest for God's Speakability*. Downers Grove, IL: InterVarsity, 2015.
Spiegelman, Willard. *How Poets See the World: The Art of Description in Contemporary Poetry*. New York: Oxford University Press, 2005.
Stout, Harry S. *The New England Soul: Preaching and Religious Culture in Colonial New England*. New York: Oxford University Press, 1986.
Stroumsa, Guy G. *A New Science: The Discovery of Religion in the Age of Reason*. Cambridge, MA: Harvard University Press, 2010.
Vigny, Alfred. "La maison du berger." *Revue des Deux Mondes* 3 (1844) 109–18.
Wesley, Charles. *The Cause and Cure of Earthquakes: A sermon Preach'd from Psalm XLIV.8*. London: Strahan, 1750.
Wesley, John. *Hymns Occasioned by the Earthquake, March 8, 1750*. London: 1750.
Wilkinson, Alan. *Dissent or Conform?: War, Peace and the English Churches 1900–1945*. London: SCM, 1986.
Williams, Rowan. "Language, Reality, Desire in Augustine's *De Doctrina*." *Journal of Literature & Theology* 3/2 (1989) 138–50.
Winthrop, John. *A Lecture on Earthquakes*. Boston: Edes and Gill, 1755.

www.ingramcontent.com/pod-product-compliance
Lightning Source LLC
Chambersburg PA
CBHW020856160426
43192CB00007B/944